GOVERNMENT PROCEDURES AND OPERATIONS

THE GOVERNMENT SHUTDOWN OF 2013

PERSPECTIVE AND ANALYSES

GOVERNMENT PROCEDURES AND OPERATIONS

Additional books in this series can be found on Nova's website under the Series tab.

Additional E-books in this series can be found on Nova's website under the E-book tab.

GOVERNMENT PROCEDURES AND OPERATIONS

THE GOVERNMENT SHUTDOWN OF 2013

PERSPECTIVE AND ANALYSES

ROSANNE C. LUNDY
EDITOR

New York

Copyright © 2014 by Nova Science Publishers, Inc.

All rights reserved. No part of this book may be reproduced, stored in a retrieval system or transmitted in any form or by any means: electronic, electrostatic, magnetic, tape, mechanical photocopying, recording or otherwise without the written permission of the Publisher.

For permission to use material from this book please contact us:
Telephone 631-231-7269; Fax 631-231-8175
Web Site: http://www.novapublishers.com

NOTICE TO THE READER

The Publisher has taken reasonable care in the preparation of this book, but makes no expressed or implied warranty of any kind and assumes no responsibility for any errors or omissions. No liability is assumed for incidental or consequential damages in connection with or arising out of information contained in this book. The Publisher shall not be liable for any special, consequential, or exemplary damages resulting, in whole or in part, from the readers' use of, or reliance upon, this material. Any parts of this book based on government reports are so indicated and copyright is claimed for those parts to the extent applicable to compilations of such works.

Independent verification should be sought for any data, advice or recommendations contained in this book. In addition, no responsibility is assumed by the publisher for any injury and/or damage to persons or property arising from any methods, products, instructions, ideas or otherwise contained in this publication.

This publication is designed to provide accurate and authoritative information with regard to the subject matter covered herein. It is sold with the clear understanding that the Publisher is not engaged in rendering legal or any other professional services. If legal or any other expert assistance is required, the services of a competent person should be sought. FROM A DECLARATION OF PARTICIPANTS JOINTLY ADOPTED BY A COMMITTEE OF THE AMERICAN BAR ASSOCIATION AND A COMMITTEE OF PUBLISHERS.

Additional color graphics may be available in the e-book version of this book.

Library of Congress Cataloging-in-Publication Data

ISBN: 978-1-63117-112-3

Published by Nova Science Publishers, Inc. † New York

Contents

Preface		vii
Chapter 1	Shutdown of the Federal Government: Causes, Processes, and Effects *Clinton T. Brass*	1
Chapter 2	Economic Activity During the Government Shutdown and Debt Limit Brinksmanship *Council of Economic Advisers*	31
Chapter 3	Impacts and Costs of the October 2013 Federal Government Shutdown *Office of Management and Budget, Executive Office of the President of the United States*	47
Chapter 4	Federal Funding Gaps: A Brief Overview *Jessica Tollestrup*	73
Chapter 5	Government Shutdown: Operations of the Department of Defense During a Lapse in Appropriations *Amy Belasco and Pat Towell*	85
Index		127

PREFACE

This book discusses the causes, processes, and effects of federal government shutdowns; economic activity during the government shutdown and debt limit brinkmanship; impacts and costs of the October 2013 federal government shutdown; a brief overview of federal funding gaps; and operations of the Department of Defense during a lapse in appropriations.

Chapter 1 – When federal agencies and programs lack appropriated funding, they experience a funding gap. Under the Antideficiency Act, they must cease operations, except in certain emergency situations or when law authorizes continued activity. Failure of the President and Congress to reach agreement on interim or full-year funding measures occasionally has caused government shutdowns, the longest of which lasted 21 full days, from December 16, 1995, to January 6, 1996. Government shutdowns have necessitated furloughs of several hundred thousand federal employees, required cessation or reduction of many government activities, and affected numerous sectors of the economy. This report discusses the causes, processes, and effects of federal government shutdowns, including potential issues for Congress.

Chapter 2 – The government shutdown and debt limit brinkmanship have had a substantial negative impact on the economy. The shutdown directly affected the economy by withdrawing government services for a sixteen day period, which not only had direct impacts but also had a range of indirect effects on the private sector. For example the travel industry was hurt by the closing of national parks, businesses in oil and gas and other industries were hurt by the cessation of permits for oil and gas drilling, the housing industry was hurt by the cessation of IRS verifications for mortgage applications, and small businesses were hurt by the shutdown of Small Business Administration loan guarantees. In addition, a reduction in consumer confidence and an increase in uncertainty associated not just with the shutdown but also the brinkmanship over the debt limit affected consumer spending, investment and hiring as well.

Chapter 3 – The October 2013 Federal government shutdown was the second longest since 1980 and the most significant on record, measured in terms of employee furlough days. Outside experts estimate that the shutdown will reduce fourth quarter Gross Domestic Product (GDP) growth by 0.2-0.6 percentage points. The Council of Economic Advisers estimates that the combination of the government shutdown and debt limit brinksmanship may have resulted in 120,000 fewer private-sector jobs created during the first two weeks of October.

This report examines the economic, budgetary, and programmatic costs of the government shutdown. These costs include economic disruption, Federal employee furloughs, programmatic impacts, other costs to the Federal budget, and impacts on the Federal workforce.

Chapter 4 – The Antideficiency Act (31 U.S.C. 1341-1342, 1511-1519) generally bars the obligation of funds in the absence of appropriations. Exceptions are made under the act, including for activities involving "the safety of human life or the protection of property." The interval during the fiscal year when appropriations for a particular project or activity are not enacted into law, either in the form of a regular appropriations act or a continuing resolution (CR), is referred to as a *funding gap*. Although funding gaps may occur at the start of the fiscal year, they also may occur any time a CR expires and another CR (or the regular appropriations bill) is not enacted immediately thereafter. Multiple funding gaps may occur within a fiscal year.

When a funding gap occurs, federal agencies are generally required to begin a *shutdown* of the affected projects and activities, which includes the prompt furlough of non-excepted personnel. The general practice of the federal government after the shutdown has ended has been to retroactively pay furloughed employees for the time they missed, as well as employees who were required to come to work.

Although a shutdown may be the result of a funding gap, the two events should be distinguished. This is because a funding gap may result in a total shutdown of all affected projects or activities in some instances, but not others. For example, when funding gaps are of a short duration, agencies may not have enough time to complete a shutdown of affected projects and activities before funding is restored. In addition, the Office of Management and Budget has previously indicated that a shutdown of agency operations within the first day of the funding gap may be postponed if a resolution appears to be imminent.

Chapter 5 – Because Congress did not provide any FY2014 funding for the Department of Defense (DOD) by October 1, 2013, the beginning of the new fiscal year, DOD, like other agencies, is now subject to a lapse in appropriations during which agencies are generally required to shut down. The Office of Management and Budget (OMB), however, has identified a number of exceptions to the requirement that agencies cease operations, including a blanket exception for activities that "provide for the national security."

With the approach of the Treasury Department's estimate of an October 17, 2013, deadline for raising the debt ceiling, concerns have grown about the potential effect on government programs and workers. If the Treasury Department were to continue the current practice of paying bills as they come due, DOD programs ranging from payments to military retirees to contractor bills could be delayed or reduced, a situation that differs from the current government shutdown. It is difficult to predict effects because of the uncertainty about Treasury actions, but payment delays could affect all programs and personnel. Negotiations are currently underway to deal with the upcoming deadline.

In: The Government Shutdown of 2013 ISBN: 978-1-63117-112-3
Editor: Rosanne C. Lundy © 2014 Nova Science Publishers, Inc.

Chapter 1

SHUTDOWN OF THE FEDERAL GOVERNMENT: CAUSES, PROCESSES, AND EFFECTS[*]

Clinton T. Brass

SUMMARY

When federal agencies and programs lack appropriated funding, they experience a funding gap. Under the Antideficiency Act, they must cease operations, except in certain emergency situations or when law authorizes continued activity. Failure of the President and Congress to reach agreement on interim or full-year funding measures occasionally has caused government shutdowns, the longest of which lasted 21 full days, from December 16, 1995, to January 6, 1996. Government shutdowns have necessitated furloughs of several hundred thousand federal employees, required cessation or reduction of many government activities, and affected numerous sectors of the economy. This report discusses the causes, processes, and effects of federal government shutdowns, including potential issues for Congress.

---

[*] This is an edited, reformatted and augmented version of a Congressional Research Service publication, CRS Report for Congress RL34680, prepared for Members and Committees of Congress, from www.crs.gov, dated September 25, 2013.

BUDGET NEGOTIATIONS AND CHOICES

It has been said that "conflict is endemic to budgeting."[1] If conflict within Congress or between Congress and the President impedes the timely enactment of annual appropriations acts or continuing resolutions, a government shutdown may occur.

Specifically, during high-stakes negotiations over appropriations measures, several options present themselves to Congress and the President. The options include

- coming to agreement on regular appropriations acts before October 1, the beginning of a new fiscal year;
- using one or more interim continuing resolutions (CRs) to extend temporary funding beyond the beginning of a fiscal year, until negotiators make final decisions about full-year funding levels; or
- not agreeing on full-year or interim appropriations acts, resulting in a funding gap and a corresponding shutdown of federal activities.

If Congress and the President pursue the second or third options, they may agree on full-year appropriations after the beginning of the fiscal year. These agreements may use a full-year CR or, more commonly, regular appropriations acts, either singly or in omnibus legislation. Congress and the President frequently agree on full-year or interim funding without coming to an impasse.[2]

On other occasions, however, Congress and the President may not come to an accommodation in time to prevent a funding gap.

This report discusses the causes of funding gaps and shutdowns of the federal government, processes that are associated with shutdowns, and how agency operations may be affected by shutdowns.[3] The report concludes with a discussion of potential issues for Congress.

CAUSES OF FEDERAL SHUTDOWNS

The federal fiscal year begins on October 1. For agencies and programs that rely on discretionary funding through annual appropriations acts, Congress and the President must enact interim or full-year appropriations by this date if many governmental activities are to continue operating.[4] If interim or full-year appropriations are not enacted into law, the time interval in which agency appropriations are not enacted is referred to as a "funding gap."[5] A funding gap also may occur any time that interim funding in a CR expires and another CR (or regular appropriations bill) is not enacted immediately thereafter.[6] When a funding gap occurs, the federal government generally begins a "shutdown" of the affected activities, including the furlough of certain personnel and curtailment of agency activities and services.[7] There are some exceptions to this process, however, as explained later in this report. Programs that are funded by laws other than annual appropriations acts (e.g., entitlements like Social Security and other mandatory spending) also may be affected by a funding gap, if program execution relies on activities that receive annually appropriated funding.

Funding gaps and government shutdowns have occurred in the past when Congress and the President did not enact regular appropriations bills by the beginning of the fiscal year.

They also have occurred when Congress and the President did not come to an agreement on stop-gap funding through a CR. As noted in another CRS report, six fairly lengthy funding gaps occurred from FY1977 to FY1980, ranging from 8 to 17 full days.[8] Subsequently, the durations of funding gaps shortened considerably.

From FY1981 to FY1995, nine funding gaps occurred with durations of up to three full days. A significant exception to the trend occurred in FY1996, when President William J. Clinton and the 104th Congress engaged in extended negotiations over budget policy. Two funding gaps and corresponding shutdowns, amounting to 5 full days and 21 full days, ensued.[9] There have been no similar funding gaps since FY1996.

The Constitution, statutory provisions, court opinions, and Department of Justice (DOJ) opinions provide the legal framework for how funding gaps and shutdowns have occurred in recent decades.[10] Article I, Section 9 of the Constitution states that "No Money shall be drawn from the Treasury, but in Consequence of Appropriations made by Law." Federal employees and contractors cannot be paid, for example, if appropriations in the first place have not been enacted.

Nevertheless, it would appear to be possible under the Constitution for the government to make contracts or other obligations if it lacked funds to pay for these commitments.[11] The so-called Antideficiency Act generally prevents this, however. The act prohibits federal officials from obligating funds before an appropriations measure has been enacted, except as authorized by law.[12]

The act also prohibits acceptance of voluntary services and employment of personal services exceeding what has been authorized by law.[13] Exceptions are made under the act to the latter prohibition for "emergencies involving the safety of human life or the protection of property." Therefore, the Antideficiency Act generally prohibits agencies from continued operation in the absence of appropriations. Failure to comply with the act may result in criminal sanctions, fines, and removal.

For years leading up to 1980, many federal agencies continued to operate during a funding gap, "minimizing all nonessential operations and obligations, believing that Congress did not intend that agencies close down," while waiting for the enactment of annual appropriations acts or continuing resolutions.[14]

In 1980 and 1981, however, U.S. Attorney General Benjamin R. Civiletti issued two opinions that more strictly interpreted the Antideficiency Act in the context of a funding gap, along with the law's exceptions.[15]

The Attorney General's opinions stated that, with some exceptions, the head of an agency could avoid violating the Antideficiency Act only by suspending the agency's operations until the enactment of an appropriation. In the absence of appropriations, exceptions would be allowed only when there is "some reasonable and articulable connection between the function to be performed and the safety of human life or the protection of property." Apart from this broad category of "human life and property" exceptions to the Antideficiency Act, the Civiletti opinions identified another broad category of exceptions: those that are "authorized by law." GAO later summarized the 1981 Civiletti opinion as identifying four sub-types of "authorized by law" exceptions.[16]

- Activities funded with appropriations of budget authority that do not expire at the end of one fiscal year, such as multiple-year and no-year appropriations (that is, when these multiple-year and no-year appropriations still have budget authority that is available for obligation at the time of a funding gap).[17]
- Activities authorized by statutes that expressly permit obligations in advance of appropriations, such as contract authority.[18]
- Activities "authorized by necessary implication from the specific terms of duties that have been imposed on, or of authorities that have been invested in, the agency." The Civiletti opinion illustrated this abstract concept by citing the situation when benefit payments under an entitlement program are funded from other-than-one-year

appropriations (i.e., where benefit payments are not subject to a funding gap, because they are authorized by permanent entitlement authority),[19] but the salaries of personnel who administer the program are funded by one-year appropriations (i.e., the salaries are subject to a funding gap). In this situation, the Attorney General offered the view that continued availability of money for benefit payments would necessarily imply that continued administration of the program is authorized by law at some level and therefore excepted from the Antideficiency Act.[20]

- Obligations "necessarily incident to presidential initiatives undertaken within his constitutional powers," such as the power to grant pardons and reprieves. GAO later expressed the view that this same rationale would apply to legislative branch agencies that incur obligations "necessary to assist the Congress in the performance of its constitutional duties."[21]

In 1990, in response to the 1981 Civiletti opinion, Congress amended 31 U.S.C. §1342 to clarify that "the term 'emergencies involving the safety of human life or the protection of property' does not include ongoing, regular functions of government the suspension of which would not imminently threaten the safety of human life or the protection of property."[22] DOJ's Office of Legal Counsel (OLC) issued a memorandum in 1995 that interpreted the effect of the amendment (hereinafter, "1995 OLC opinion").[23] The 1995 OLC opinion said one aspect of the 1981 Civiletti opinion's description of emergency governmental functions should be modified in light of the amendment, but that the 1981 opinion otherwise "continues to be a sound analysis of the legal authorities respecting government operations" during a funding gap.[24]

More recently, the Office of Management and Budget (OMB) summarized its interpretation of exceptions to the Antideficiency Act in memoranda that were issued to agencies in April and December 2011 (regarding FY2011 and FY2012 annual appropriations, respectively), and September 2013 (regarding FY2014 annual appropriations).[25]

Observers sometimes wish to contrast the effect of a government shutdown, on one hand, with the effect of the federal government reaching its statutory debt limit and not raising it, on the other. The two situations are distinct in terms of their effects on agency operations and federal government payments to liquidate obligations (see box).[26]

> **Distinction between a Government Shutdown
> and a Debt Limit Impasse**
>
> In a government shutdown situation, Congress and the President do not enact interim or full-year appropriations for an agency. In this case, the agency does not have budget authority available for obligation for things like salaries or rent. Under the Antideficiency Act, the agency may obligate some funds in certain "excepted" areas, but these obligations are highly restricted. As a consequence, the agency must shut down non-excepted activities, and the federal government may not make actual payment for excepted or non-excepted activities until budget authority is provided.
>
> In a debt limit impasse, by contrast, the government no longer has an ability to borrow to finance its obligations. As a result, the federal government would need to rely solely on incoming revenues to finance obligations. If this occurred during a period when the federal government was running a deficit, the dollar amount of newly incurred federal obligations would exceed the dollar amount of newly incoming revenues. In such a situation, an agency may continue to obligate funds, because it has budget authority available for obligation, provided that appropriations are in place. However, the Treasury Department may not be able to liquidate all obligations that result in federal outlays, due to a shortage of cash, which may result in delays in federal payments and disruptions in government operations.

OMB AND AGENCY SHUTDOWN PROCESSES

OMB provides executive branch agencies with instructions on how to prepare for and operate during a funding gap in its annually revised *Circular No. A-11*.[27] The circular cites the two Civiletti opinions and the 1995 OLC opinion as background and guidance. The circular establishes two "policies" regarding the absence of appropriations:

- a prohibition on incurring obligations unless the obligations are otherwise authorized by law and

- permission to incur obligations "as necessary for orderly termination of an agency's functions," but prohibition of any disbursement (i.e., payment).

The circular also directs agency heads to develop and maintain shutdown plans. Prior to the 2011 revision of *Circular No. A-11*, the circular broadly indicated that the plans were to be submitted to OMB when initially prepared and also when revised. The plans themselves were required to contain summary information about the number of employees expected to be on-board before a shutdown and also the number of employees who would be "retained" (i.e., excepted from furlough) during a shutdown. With the August 2011 revision of the circular, however, OMB newly required that these plans contain more detailed information, be updated under certain conditions, and be updated at a minimum on a four-year schedule, starting August 1, 2014. OMB's change in instructions occurred four months after Congress and the President almost came to an impasse in April 2011, on FY2011 appropriations. At the time, OMB instructed agencies to create or revise shutdown plans and to post them publicly on the Internet shortly before funding was scheduled to expire.[28] Because no shutdown occurred, however, it is not clear what the effects of a shutdown would have been under these plans.

Under OMB's current instructions from *Circular No. A-11*, agency heads are to use the DOJ opinions and the circular, in consultation with the agencies' general counsels, to "decide what agency activities are excepted or otherwise legally authorized to continue during an appropriations hiatus."[29] Furthermore, plans are to address agency actions in two distinct time windows of a shutdown: an initial period of one to five days, which OMB characterized as a "short" hiatus, and a second period if a shutdown were to continue. Among other things, a shutdown plan is required to include

- a summary of agency activities that will continue and those that will cease;
- an estimate of the time to complete the shutdown, to the nearest half-day;
- the number of employees expected to be on-board (i.e., filled positions) before implementation of the plan;
- the total number of employees to be retained, broken out into five categories of exceptions to the Antideficiency Act,[30] including employees
1. who are paid from a resource other than annual appropriations;

2. who are necessary to perform activities expressly authorized by law;
3. who are necessary to perform activities necessarily implied by law;
4. who are necessary to the discharge of the President's constitutional duties and powers; and
5. who are necessary to protect life and property.

After a plan provides this information for an agency as a whole, the plan is required to further break out some of the information by major "component" (e.g., bureau-size entity within a department).

In general, the OMB circular refers to employees who are to be furloughed as "released," and employees who will not be furloughed as "retained" or "excepted."[31] OMB's circular also instructs agencies to take personnel actions to release employees according to applicable law and Office of Personnel Management (OPM) regulations.[32]

OMB documents and guidance from previous funding gaps and shutdowns may provide insights into current and future practices. OPM has provided links to, and retyped copies of, previous OMB bulletins and memoranda for reference.[33] These and other OMB documents also have been reproduced in several legislative branch documents.[34]

EFFECTS OF A FEDERAL GOVERNMENT SHUTDOWN

Effects on Federal Officials and Employees

Effects of a shutdown may occur

- in anticipation of a potential funding gap (e.g., planning),
- during an actual gap (e.g., furlough and curtailed operations), and
- afterwards (e.g., working to reduce accumulated backlogs of work).

An immediate shutdown effect is the "shutdown furlough" of certain federal employees—that is, placement of the employees in a temporary, nonduty, nonpay status.[35] Shutdown furloughs are not considered a break in service and are generally creditable for retaining benefits and seniority.

There appears to be no guarantee that employees placed on shutdown furlough would receive pay for the time they are placed on furlough. This may be the case, because if furloughed employees are prohibited from coming to work during a shutdown, the government arguably would not be incurring a legal obligation to pay them. Several considerations, including personnel costs, future productivity, and retention, might be weighed when assessing the issue of retroactive pay for furloughed staff. However, in the case of excepted employees, OMB has stated several times in detailed, shutdown-related guidance to agencies that

> [w]ithout further specific direction or enactment by Congress, all excepted employees are entitled to receive payment for obligations incurred by their agencies for their performance of excepted work during the period of the appropriations lapse. After appropriations are enacted, payroll centers will pay all excepted employees for time worked.[36]

Nevertheless, in historical practice, federal employees who have been furloughed under a shutdown (i.e., those who were not excepted) generally have received their salaries retroactively as a result of legislation to that effect.[37]

As noted earlier, the two most recent funding gaps and corresponding shutdowns occurred in FY1996.[38] The first, which lasted five full days between November 13-19, 1995, resulted in the furlough of approximately 800,000 federal employees.[39] It was caused by the expiration of a continuing resolution agreed to on September 30, 1995 (P.L. 104-31), and by President Clinton's veto of a second continuing resolution.[40] The second FY1996 partial shutdown of the federal government lasted 21 full days between December 15, 1995, and January 6, 1996.[41] The shutdown was triggered by the expiration of a continuing resolution enacted on November 20, 1995 (P.L. 104-56), which funded the government through December 15, 1995. On January 2, 1996, the estimate of furloughed federal employees was 284,000.[42] Another 475,000 excepted federal employees continued to work in nonpay status. There was a total of eight continuing resolutions from January 6, 1996, until April 26, 1996, when the Omnibus Consolidated Rescissions and Appropriations Act of 1996 (P.L. 104-134) was enacted. This consolidated appropriations act provided budget authority for agencies and programs not covered in the FY1996 annual appropriations acts that had already become law. A graphical depiction of the FY1996 appropriations process, including the two funding gaps, is available in another CRS report.[43]

Executive Branch

Among the three branches of the federal government, the executive branch is the largest in number of personnel and size of budgets. Several types of executive branch officials and employees are not subject to furlough. These include the President, presidential appointees, and federal employees deemed "excepted."[44] OPM has described "excepted" employees, who are required to work during a shutdown, as "employees who are funded through annual appropriations who are nonetheless excepted from the furlough because they are performing work that, by law, may continue to be performed during a lapse in appropriations."[45] Nevertheless, excepted employees who are normally paid from annual appropriations would not receive pay during the shutdown period.

Legislative Branch[46]

Due to their constitutional responsibilities and a permanent appropriation for congressional pay, Members of Congress are not subject to furlough.[47]

During a funding gap, congressional employees whose pay is disbursed by the Secretary of the Senate or the Chief Administrative Officer of the House of Representatives would not be paid if there is no appropriation to fund legislative branch activities. Any decision regarding requirements that a congressional employee continue to work during a government shutdown would appear to fall to his or her employing authority.[48] Activities of legislative branch agencies would likely also be restricted, in consultation with Congress, to activities required to support Congress with its constitutional responsibilities or those necessary to protect life and property.[49]

Judicial Branch[50]

If a funding gap had occurred in FY2013, the judiciary would have continued to operate using funds derived from court filing and other fees and from no-year appropriations.[51] The judiciary estimated that these funds, if used cautiously, could have sustained judiciary activities for approximately 10 working days after an appropriations lapse.[52]

If a lapse in appropriations were to continue to exist after various fee balances like these were exhausted, the judiciary would continue to operate under the terms of the Antideficiency Act, which the judiciary said allows "essential work" to continue during a lapse in appropriations.[53] Such "essential work" includes powers exercised by the judiciary under the Constitution, including activities that support the exercise of Article III judicial powers (i.e., the resolution of cases).[54] Consequently, in the judicial branch, judges would not be subject to furlough, nor would core court staff and probation and pretrial services officers whose service is considered essential to the continued resolution of cases. Each court would be responsible for determining the number of court staff and officers needed to support the exercise of its Article III judicial powers.[55] Such staff performing "essential work" functions would report to work in a non-pay status while other staff would be furloughed.[56]

Protected by a constitutional prohibition against a diminution in their pay, Supreme Court Justices and other Article III judges would continue to be paid during a lapse in appropriations.[57] Also, in the judiciary's view, other judicial officers, such as U.S. Claims Court judges, U.S. magistrate judges, and U.S. bankruptcy judges, would continue to be paid as well. Staff, however, would not be paid until Congress enacts an appropriation.[58]

Examples of Excepted Activities and Personnel

Previous determinations of excepted activities and personnel would not necessarily hold for any future shutdown. However, past experience may inform future OMB and agency decisions. The near-impasses in April and December 2011 regarding enactment of FY2011 and FY2012 annual appropriations, respectively, resulted in executive branch agencies posting a substantial amount of information on the Internet about their plans for a potential shutdown, including information about excepted and non-excepted personnel and activities.[59] In September 2013, in the context of FY2014 annual appropriations, OMB directed agencies to update these plans and prepare for their potential release.[60] These plans might provide insight into questions of whether government activities at specific agencies and programs, and in specific situations, would continue or cease, at least according to interpretations of law at the time.

More generally, OMB memoranda may provide insights into which activities and personnel might be considered to be excepted. In April and December 2011, then-OMB Director Jacob J. Lew outlined several categories of exceptions to the Antideficiency Act and provided further explanation on how agencies should interpret the categories.[61] OMB Director Sylvia M. Burwell provided similar guidance in September 2013.[62] Three decades earlier, an OMB memorandum of November 17, 1981, from Director David A. Stockman to the heads of executive agencies, identified "examples of excepted activities."[63] The memorandum, which still was in effect for the FY1996 shutdowns, explained Beginning [on the first day of the appropriations hiatus], agencies may continue activities otherwise authorized by law, those that protect life and property and those necessary to begin phasedown of other activities. Primary examples of activities agencies may continue are those which may be found under applicable statutes to:

1. Provide for the national security, including the conduct of foreign relations essential to the national security or the safety of life and property.
2. Provide for benefit payments and the performance of contract obligations under no-year or multi-year or other funds remaining available for those purposes.
3. Conduct essential activities to the extent that they protect life and property, including:
   a. Medical care of inpatients and emergency outpatient care;
   b. Activities essential to ensure continued public health and safety, including safe use of food and drugs and safe use of hazardous materials;
   c. The continuance of air traffic control and other transportation safety functions and the protection of transport property;
   d. Border and coastal protection and surveillance;
   e. Protection of Federal lands, buildings, waterways, equipment and other property owned by the United States;
   f. Care of prisoners and other persons in the custody of the United States;
   g. Law enforcement and criminal investigations;
   h. Emergency and disaster assistance;
   i. Activities essential to the preservation of the essential elements of the money and banking system of the United States, including borrowing and tax collection activities of the Treasury;
   j. Activities that ensure production of power and maintenance of the power distribution system; and
   k. Activities necessary to maintain protection of research property.

You should maintain the staff and support services necessary to continue these essential functions.

Effects on Government Operations and Services to the Public

Illustrations from FY1996 Shutdowns

The effects of the two FY1996 shutdowns on government activities and the public received extensive attention. Although the effects on the public of any future shutdown would not necessarily reflect past experience, past events may be illustrative of effects that are possible.[64] Several examples follow that were reported in congressional hearings, news media, and agency accounts, about the operations and services of executive branch agencies.[65]

- *Health.* New patients were not accepted into clinical research at the National Institutes of Health (NIH) clinical center; the Centers for Disease Control and Prevention ceased disease surveillance; and hotline calls to NIH concerning diseases were not answered.[66]
- *Law Enforcement and Public Safety.* Delays occurred in the processing of alcohol, tobacco, firearms, and explosives applications by the Bureau of Alcohol, Tobacco, and Firearms; work on more than 3,500 bankruptcy cases reportedly was suspended; cancellation of the recruitment and testing of federal law-enforcement officials reportedly occurred, including the hiring of 400 border patrol agents; and delinquent child-support cases were delayed.[67]
- *Parks, Museums, and Monuments.* Closure of 368 National Park Service sites (loss of 7 million visitors) reportedly occurred, with loss of tourism revenues to local communities; and closure of national museums and monuments (reportedly with an estimated loss of 2 million visitors) occurred.[68]
- *Visas and Passports.* Approximately 20,000-30,000 applications by foreigners for visas reportedly went unprocessed each day; 200,000 U.S. applications for passports reportedly went unprocessed; and U.S. tourist industries and airlines reportedly sustained millions of dollars in losses.[69]
- *American Veterans.* Multiple services were curtailed, ranging from health and welfare to finance and travel.[70]
- *Federal Contractors.* Of $18 billion in Washington, DC, area contracts, $3.7 billion (over 20%) reportedly were affected adversely by the funding lapse; the National Institute of Standards and Technology (NIST) was unable to issue a new standard for lights and lamps that was scheduled to be effective January 1, 1996, possibly

resulting in delayed product delivery and lost sales; and employees of federal contractors reportedly were furloughed without pay.[71]

In a February 1996 letter, OMB provided other information about the FY1996 shutdowns. The information, which later was included in a congressional hearing print, included a list of effects from the shutdowns, lists of agencies and corresponding numbers of employees who were said to be excepted or not excepted from furlough, and a cost estimate of $1.4 billion for the shutdowns.[72]

During the FY1996 government shutdowns,[73] the federal courts generally operated with limited disruption to their personnel.[74] In the absence of appropriated funds, the judiciary used fee revenues and "carryover" funds from prior years to support what it considered its essential function of hearing and deciding cases.[75] Internal judiciary guidelines, according to the official publication of the U.S. courts, recognized the "unique function of the Judiciary" and anticipated that all activities "essential to maintain and support the exercise of the judicial power of the United States during a funding lapse" would continue.[76] The funding lapse, however, did affect some court functions, with some judges entertaining motions for continuances in civil cases and at least one district court announcing it would not start any new civil jury trials. An appellate court, it also was reported, had to reschedule several arguments because government lawyers were unable to attend. During the November 1995 government shutdown, lack of funding resulted in furloughs of most of the staff of the federal judiciary's two support agencies, the Federal Judicial Center and the Administrative Office of the U.S. Courts.[77] During the second shutdown, prior to the judiciary's decision to use fee revenues and carryover funds to continue essential functions, some courts did furlough personnel "on a limited basis."[78]

Effects on Mandatory Spending Programs

Programs that are funded by laws other than annual appropriations acts—for example, some entitlement programs—may, or may not, be affected by a funding gap. Specific circumstances appear to be significant. For example, although the funds needed to make payments to beneficiaries may be available automatically pursuant to permanent appropriations, the payments may be processed by employees who are paid with funds provided in annual appropriations acts. In such situations, the question arises whether a mandatory program can continue to function during a funding gap, if appropriations were not enacted to pay salaries of administering employees. As noted earlier in this report, according to the 1981 Civiletti opinion, at least some of these employees would not be subject to furlough, because authority to continue administration of a program could be inferred from Congress's direction that benefit payments continue to be made according to an entitlement formula.[79] That is, obligating funds for the salaries of these personnel would be excepted from the Antideficiency Act's restrictions during a funding gap. However, such a determination would depend upon the absence of contrary legislative history in specific circumstances.

Nevertheless, the experience of the Social Security Administration (SSA) during the FY1996 shutdowns illustrates what might happen over a period of time in these situations. The lack of funds for some employees' salaries, for example, may impinge eventually on the processing and payment of new entitlement claims. SSA's administrative history describes how 4,780 employees were allowed to be retained during the initial stages of the first shutdown.[80] The majority of these employees were "in direct service positions to ensure the continuance of benefits to currently enrolled Social Security, SSI and Black Lung beneficiaries." Avoidance of furloughs was possible, because "appropriations were available to fund the program costs of paying benefits, [which] implied authority to incur obligations for the costs necessary to administer those benefits." SSA furloughed its remaining 61,415 employees. Before long, however, SSA and OMB reconsidered. SSA had not retained staff to, among other things, respond to "telephone calls from customers needing a Social Security card to work or who needed to change the address where their check should be mailed for the following month." SSA then advised OMB that the agency would need to retain 49,715 additional employees for direct service work, including the processing of new claims for Social Security benefits. Further adjustments were made during the considerably longer second shutdown, in response to increasing difficulties in administering the agency's entitlement programs.

More Recent Prospective Statements and Analyses

In 2011, the federal judiciary commented about the potential consequences of a shutdown on its operations and services.[81] According to a judiciary press release, in the event of a funding lapse for FY2011 appropriations, the judiciary was prepared to keep the federal courts operating for about two weeks by using non-appropriated funds (as it did during the 1995-1996 government shutdowns).[82] However, once that funding was exhausted, the federal court system would face "serious disruptions." At that point, federal courts, "following their own contingency plans," would "limit operations to essential activities":

> For the federal courts, this would mean limiting activities to those functions necessary and essential to continue the resolution of cases. All other personnel services not related to judicial functions would be suspended.
> The jury system would operate as necessary, although payments to jurors would be deferred. Attorneys and essential support staff in federal defender offices and court-appointed counsel would continue to provide defense services as needed, but again, payments would be deferred. Courts would determine the number of probation office staff needed to maintain service to the courts and the safety of the community.[83]

The judiciary also advised judges and court unit executives, in the event of a funding lapse, to post information on their individual court websites about what operations would continue during and after the initial two-week period.[84]

Most executive branch agencies posted shutdown plans on OMB's website in April and December 2011, as noted earlier in this report, in anticipation of potential shutdowns related to FY2011 and FY2012 funding.[85] With regard to the plans, most agencies created both a Web page describing shutdown procedures as well as distributable PDF documents. The resources covered many topics in addition to information that OMB *Circular No. A-11* required about excepted and non-excepted employees. Additional topics included shutdown precedents, guidelines, furlough policies, and frequently asked questions. Documents also addressed availability of government services, unemployment compensation for federal employees, union concerns, and information about past shutdowns. As noted earlier, in September 2013, OMB directed agencies to update these plans and prepare for their potential release, in the context of FY2014 annual appropriations.[86] Some prospective analyses also have been conducted in specific policy areas. For example, CRS issued a report that analyzes government procurement in times of fiscal uncertainty. The report provides an overview of the various options that the government has, pursuant to the terms of its contracts or otherwise, when confronted with actual or potential funding gaps, funding shortfalls, or budget cuts.[87] During the near-impasse on FY2011 appropriations in April 2011, another CRS analysis examined the potential effects of a shutdown on Department of Defense (DOD) operations and personnel.[88]

POTENTIAL ISSUES FOR CONGRESS

Quality and Specificity of Agency Planning

In December 1995, Representative John L. Mica, chairman of the Subcommittee on Civil Service of the House Committee on Government Reform and Oversight, convened a hearing that focused on the first FY1996 shutdown and potential implications for the future.[89] Among other things, then-Chairman Mica raised concerns about the shutdown's planning and execution by agencies and OMB, saying "the execution of the shutdown was, in many instances, disorganized and illogical, at best, and oftentimes chaotic experience."[90] As an example, he cited the "recall of more than 50,000 Social Security personnel [three days into the furlough], raising questions about whether they should have been furloughed in the first place."[91] In addition, then-Ranking Member James P. Moran expressed interest in clarifying the distinction between excepted and non-excepted activities and employees. If similar issues were currently of concern, Congress might consider lawmaking and oversight options related to the quality and specificity of agency shutdown planning. The shutdown plans that agencies released in April and December 2011, in the wake of negotiations on FY2011 and FY2012 appropriations, might provide a starting point for such attention.

Availability of Updated Agency Shutdown Plans

OMB's *Circular No. A-11* requires executive agencies to submit to OMB "plans for an orderly shutdown in the event of the absence of appropriations."[92] OMB has required the development and maintenance of these shutdown plans since 1980. Prior to the circular's 2011 revision, the circular broadly indicated that the plans were to be submitted to OMB when initially prepared and also when revised. With the August 2011 revision of the circular, however, OMB newly required that these shutdown plans be updated whenever there is a change in the source of funding for an agency program, or "any significant modification, expansion, or reduction in agency program activities."[93] In any case, plans are required to be updated and submitted to OMB with a minimum frequency of once every four years, starting August 1, 2014.

The April and December 2011 releases of agency shutdown plans on the Internet—on OMB's website and on agency websites—brought a new level of transparency to agency shutdown planning. However, each release occurred on the final day of funding availability before an interim CR was scheduled to expire, and in the context of negotiations where an impasse seemed to many observers to be a possibility. Before the April 2011 release, it was not clear the extent to which agency shutdown plans ever had been made publicly available or systematically shared with Congress and agency stakeholders for scrutiny and feedback. It remains to be seen over time whether these shutdown plans will remain a permanent fixture of federal agency and OMB websites. Similarly, it is not clear if any updated plans will be made available to Congress and the public, except at a time determined by OMB or a sitting President. Scrutiny over agency shutdown plans may provide incentives for agencies to improve the quality of the plans, should it become necessary at some point for agencies to execute the plans, and may inform budget policy debates about the potential impacts of shutdowns. On the other hand, such inquiries may distract agency personnel from other duties and raise sensitive issues regarding what activities and employees should be considered to be excepted from Antideficiency Act restrictions.

Possible National Security Implications[94]

A federal government shutdown could have possible negative security implications,[95] as some entities wishing to take actions harmful to U.S. interests may see the nation as physically and politically vulnerable.[96] The Antideficiency Act is silent regarding which specific organizations would be excepted in whole or part from a government shutdown. The act's provisions and historical guidance from OMB, however, suggest that entities that perform a national security function may be allowed to continue many of their operations.[97] Historically, individuals responsible for supporting the nation's global security activities, public safety efforts, and foreign relations pursuits have been excepted from furloughs that accompany a government shutdown.[98]

The actions that are taken in anticipation of a government shutdown may lessen the negative effects of an incident of national security significance occurring during this period. How agencies and OMB prepare for a government shutdown may have short- and long-term consequences if an incident occurs during a period of reduction in government services or soon after a resumption of all government activities. Should federal government organizations traditionally not viewed as an excepted part of the security apparatus be shut down, and subsequently become needed during a crisis or emerging situation, the nation's ability to respond to an incident could be delayed. Such a situation could result in increased risk to the nation and a longer recovery time as services and support activities normally provided to non-federal entities may not be available when needed. Some security observers may offer concerns that the longer the duration of a government shutdown, the more at-risk the nation becomes as enemies of the U.S. may seek to exploit perceived vulnerabilities.

End Notes

[1] Irene S. Rubin, "Understanding the Role of Conflict in Budgeting," in Roy T. Meyers, ed., Handbook of Government Budgeting (San Francisco: Jossey-Bass, 1999), p. 30.

[2] For discussion, see CRS Report RL32614, Duration of Continuing Resolutions in Recent Years, by Jessica Tollestrup. For analysis of the potential functions and impacts of CRs, see CRS Report R42647, Continuing Resolutions: Overview of Components and Recent Practices, by Jessica Tollestrup; and CRS Report RL34700, Interim Continuing Resolutions (CRs): Potential Impacts on Agency Operations, by Clinton T. Brass. For more detailed discussion of the potential impacts of CRs, see CRS Congressional Distribution Memorandum, Potential Impacts of Interim Continuing Resolutions (CRs) on Agency Operations and the Functioning of the Federal Government, coordinated by Clinton T. Brass, July 8, 2008 (available on request).

[3] This report focuses on funding gaps and shutdowns that are associated with annual appropriations acts. It does not focus on shutdowns that may occur when a specific program or agency is funded by legislation other than annual appropriations acts, and the statutory authorization for the program or agency expires. Nevertheless, these "expired authorization" shutdowns are similar in many ways to broader "annual appropriations" shutdowns. An example of an expired authorization shutdown occurred in early 2010, when authorization for certain surface transportation programs and trust funds expired after 11:59 p.m. on February 28, 2010. The expiration caused a lapse in authority to expend funds that, among other things, affected certain construction projects on federal lands and required nearly 2,000 U.S. Department of Transportation employees to be furloughed. On March 2, 2010, P.L. 111-144 reauthorized these activities (124 Stat. 45). On April 15, 2010, P.L. 111-157 provided compensation to furloughed federal employees and ratified retroactively all "essential actions" taken during the lapse by federal employees, contractors, and grantees to "protect life and property and to bring about orderly termination of Government functions" (124 Stat. 1118).

[4] Discretionary funding generally refers to budget authority (i.e., the authority to incur financial obligations that result in government expenditures) that is provided in and controlled by an annual appropriations act. Conversely, mandatory funding generally refers to budget authority that is provided in and controlled by laws other than annual appropriations acts. Some budget authority provided in annual appropriations acts for certain programs is treated as mandatory, however, because the relevant authorizing legislation entitles beneficiaries to receive payment or otherwise obligates the government to make payment. See U.S. Government Accountability Office (formerly the General Accounting Office; hereinafter

GAO), A Glossary of Terms Used in the Federal Budget Process, GAO-05-734SP, September 2005, pp. 46, 66; and CRS Report RS20129, Entitlements and Appropriated Entitlements in the Federal Budget Process, by Bill Heniff Jr.

[5] CRS Report RS20348, Federal Funding Gaps: A Brief Overview, by Jessica Tollestrup. Some observers use alternative terms "lapse in appropriations" and "appropriations hiatus" instead of "funding gap."

[6] The Office of Management and Budget (OMB) effectively has taken the view that if funding authority expires at the end of a day (e.g., Friday, April 8, 2011), but continuing or full-year authority is enacted at any time during the next day (e.g., Saturday, April 9, 2011; where enacted means signed by the President after passing both chambers of Congress), no funding gap or shutdown occurs. See OMB Memorandum M-11-13, Planning for Agency Operations During a Lapse in Government Funding, April 7, 2011, p. 3, and OMB Memorandum M-11-14, Anticipated Enactment of a Continuing Resolution, April 8, 2011, p. 1, at http://www.whitehouse.gov/omb/memoranda_default/.

[7] Although a shutdown may be the result of a funding gap, the two events should be distinguished. This is because a funding gap may result in a total shutdown of all affected projects or activities in some instances, but not in others. For example, if a funding gap is of a short duration, agencies may not have enough time to complete a shutdown of affected projects and activities before funding is restored. In addition, OMB has previously indicated that a shutdown of agency operations within the first day of a funding gap may be postponed if it appears that a CR or regular appropriations bill is likely to be enacted on the first day of a funding gap. See ibid.

[8] CRS Report RS20348, Federal Funding Gaps: A Brief Overview, by Jessica Tollestrup. These funding gaps occurred before the Department of Justice issued opinions in 1980 and 1981 about allowable agency activities during a funding gap. The opinions, which are discussed later, were restrictive in their implications about allowable agency activities compared to what agencies had done in the past during a funding gap.

[9] For a detailed chronology and graphical depiction of the FY1996 appropriations process, including the two funding gaps, see CRS Report RS20348, Federal Funding Gaps: A Brief Overview, by Jessica Tollestrup.

[10] For legal analysis of funding gaps, see GAO, Principles of Federal Appropriations Law, 3rd ed., vol. II, GAO-06-382SP, February 2006, chapter 6, pp. 6-146 - 6-159.

[11] For discussion, see prepared statement of Walter Dellinger, Assistant Attorney General, in U.S. Congress, Senate Committee on the Budget and House Committee on the Budget, Effects of Potential Government Shutdown, hearing, 104th Cong., 1st sess., September 19, 1995, S.Hrg. 104-175 (Washington: GPO, 1995), p. 18. Some commentators, however, have expressed a contrary view. See Jim Schweiter and Herb Fenster, Government Contract Funding under Continuing Resolutions, 95 Fed. Cont. Rep. 180, note 17 (February 15, 2011).

[12] 31 U.S.C. §1341. The Antideficiency Act (31 U.S.C. §§1341-1342, §§1511-1519) is discussed in CRS Report RL30795, General Management Laws: A Compendium, by Clinton T. Brass et al., pp. 93-97. GAO provides information on the act, at http://www.gao.gov/legal/lawresources/antideficiencybackground.html.

[13] 31 U.S.C. §1342; see also §1515.

[14] U.S. GAO, Funding Gaps Jeopardize Federal Government Operations, PAD-81-31, March 3, 1981, pp. i, 2, at http://archive.gao.gov/f0102/114835.pdf.

[15] 43 Op. Att'y Gen. 224 (Apr. 25, 1980), 43 Op. Att'y Gen. 293 (January 16, 1981). The Civiletti opinions are included in a GAO report as Appendices IV and VIII. See U.S. GAO,

Funding Gaps Jeopardize Federal Government Operations, PAD-81-31, March 3, 1981, at http://www.gao.gov/assets/140/132616.pdf. For a detailed discussion of exceptions to the Antideficiency Act, see U.S. GAO, Principles of Federal Appropriations Law, vol. II, pp. 6-146 - 6- 159.

[16] The bulleted text here draws, in part, from ibid., pp. 6-149 – 6-150. GAO also noted that the courts have added to the list of exceptions to the Antideficiency Act in certain circumstances (ibid., p. 6-152).

[17] The term "multiple-year budget authority" refers to budget authority that remains available for obligation for a fixed period of time in excess of one fiscal year. The term "no-year budget authority" refers to budget authority that remains available for an indefinite period of time (e.g., "to remain available until expended"). See GAO, A Glossary of Terms Used in the Federal Budget Process, GAO-05-734SP, September 2005, p. 22. In addition, agencies that receive most or all of their budget authority for their day-to-day operations through means that are not dependent on appropriations acts, such as the U.S. Postal Service and the Bureau of Consumer Financial Protection in the Federal Reserve System, would fall under this exception.

[18] For explanation of contract authority, see ibid., p. 21.

[19] In such a case, budget authority is available to make payments as a result of previously enacted legislation and is available without further legislative action. "Entitlement authority" refers to authority to make payments (including loans and grants) for which budget authority is not provided in advance by appropriations acts to any person or government if, under the provisions of the law containing such authority, the federal government is legally required to make the payments to persons or governments that meet the requirements established by law. See ibid., pp. 22-23 and 47.

[20] See the section of this report titled "Effects on Mandatory Spending Programs" for more detailed discussion.

[21] U.S. GAO, Principles of Federal Appropriations Law, vol. II, p. 6-150.

[22] Ibid., p. 6-151, citing P.L. 101-508, 104 Stat. 1388, at 1388-621 (now codified at 31 U.S.C. §1342).

[23] U.S. Department of Justice, Office of Legal Counsel, Government Operations in the Event of a Lapse in Appropriations, memorandum from Walter Dellinger, Assistant Attorney General, for Alice Rivlin, Director, Office of Management and Budget, August 16, 1995, reprinted in U.S. Congress, Senate Committee on the Budget and House Committee on the Budget, Effects of Potential Government Shutdown, hearing, 104th Cong., 1st sess., September 19, 1995, S.Hrg. 104-175 (Washington: GPO, 1995), pp. 77-85.

[24] Ibid., p. 78. In light of the intervening amendments, the 1995 OLC opinion required the safety of human life or the protection of property to be compromised "in some significant degree" in order for a function to be considered excepted.

[25] OMB Memorandum M-11-13, Planning for Agency Operations During a Lapse in Government Funding, April 7, 2011, pp. 4-6; OMB Memorandum M-12-03, Planning for Agency Operations During a Lapse in Government Funding, December 15, 2011, Attachment 1 (first three pages of non-paginated attachment); and OMB Memorandum M-13-22, Planning for Agency Operations During a Potential Lapse in Appropriations, September 17, 2013, pp. 3-5.

[26] For further discussion of the federal debt limit, see CRS Report R41633, Reaching the Debt Limit: Background and Potential Effects on Government Operations, coordinated by Mindy R. Levit.

[27] U.S. Executive Office of the President, Office of Management and Budget (hereinafter OMB), Circular No. A-11: Preparation, Submission, and Execution of the Budget, July 2013, Section 124, at http://www.whitehouse.gov/omb/ circulars_a11_current_year_a11_toc. See also CRS Report RS21665, Office of Management and Budget (OMB): A Brief Overview, by Clinton T. Brass.

[28] On April 8, 2011, OMB began to post on its website links to the shutdown plans that agencies and the Executive Office of the President developed under the 2010 version of Circular No. A-11. For the website, see OMB, "Agency Contingency Plans," at http://www.white house.gov/omb/contingency-plans. The posting occurred shortly before funding from an interim CR was due to expire at the end of the day. The FY2011 appropriations impasse was avoided before midnight with enactment of another interim CR (P.L. 112-8) and an announcement that the outline of an agreement had been reached on how to provide full-year funding for FY2011. A week later, with the enactment of P.L. 112-10, Congress and the President agreed on full-year funding for all 12 regular appropriations bills. OMB posted revised shutdown plans from many agencies on its website in December 2011, when Congress and the President neared a potential impasse on FY2012 funding. For OMB's guidance to agencies related to FY2012 funding, see OMB Memorandum M-12-03, Planning for Agency Operations During a Lapse in Government Funding, December 15, 2011.

[29] OMB, Circular No. A-11, July 2013, Section 124.1.

[30] OMB provided guidance to help agencies interpret categories like these in memoranda that were issued during the near-impasses on FY2011 appropriations (in April 2011), FY2012 appropriations (in December 2011), and FY2014 appropriations (in September 2013). See, respectively, OMB Memorandum M-11-13, Planning for Agency Operations During a Lapse in Government Funding, April 7, 2011, pp. 4-6; OMB Memorandum M-12-03, Planning for Agency Operations During a Lapse in Government Funding, December 15, 2011, Attachment 1 (first three pages of non-paginated attachment); and OMB Memorandum M-13-22, Planning for Agency Operations During a Potential Lapse in Appropriations, September 17, 2013, pp. 3-5.

[31] In congressional hearings that focused on the first FY1996 shutdown, some witnesses expressed regret that the terms "nonessential" and "essential" had been used to describe employees subject to furlough, and not subject to furlough, respectively. Use of the term "nonessential" was demeaning, they suggested. See U.S. Congress, House Committee on Government Reform and Oversight, Subcommittee on Civil Service, Government Shutdown I: What's Essential? hearings, 104th Cong., 1st sess., December 6 and 14, 1995 (Washington: GPO, 1997), pp. 48, 228-229, at http://www.archive.org/details/ governments hutdo00unit.

[32] OPM maintains a website with guidance, historical OMB and DOJ documents, and frequently asked questions about furloughs, at http://www.opm.gov/policy-data-oversight/pay-leave/furlough-guidance/.

[33] See ibid. The reproduced OMB documents include, in chronological order: OMB Bulletin No. 80-14, Shutdown of Agency Operations Upon Failure by the Congress to Enact Appropriations, August 28, 1980 (citing the 1980 Civiletti opinion and requiring agencies to develop shutdown plans); OMB Memorandum, Agency Operations in the Absence of Appropriations, November 17, 1981 (referencing OMB Bulletin No. 80-14; saying the 1981 Civiletti opinion remains in effect; and providing examples of "excepted activities" that may be continued under a funding gap); OMB Bulletin No. 80-14, Supplement No. 1, Agency Operations in the Absence of Appropriations, August 20, 1982 ("updating" OMB

Bulletin No. 80-14 and newly requiring agencies to submit contingency plans for review by OMB); OMB Memorandum M-91-02, Agency Operations in the Absence of Appropriations, October 5, 1990 (referencing OMB Bulletin No. 80-14; stating that OMB Bulletin No. 80-14 was "amended" by the OMB Memorandum of November 17, 1981; saying the 1981 Civiletti opinion remains in effect; and directing agencies on a Friday how to handle a funding gap that begins during the weekend); OMB Memorandum M-95-18, Agency Plans for Operations During Funding Hiatus, August 22, 1995 (referencing OMB Bulletin No. 80-14, as amended; citing the 1981 Civiletti opinion; transmitting to agencies the 1995 OLC opinion as an "update" to the 1981 Civiletti opinion; and directing agencies to send updated contingency plans to OMB); OMB Circular No. A-11, Section 124, July 2013 (mislabeled online as linking to the August 2011 version of the circular) (providing annually issued guidance to agencies on shutdown-related topics); and OMB Memorandum M-13-22, Planning for Agency Operations During a Potential Lapse in Appropriations, September 17, 2013 (referring to Circular No. A-11, OLC legal opinions, and OPM Web guidance; providing detailed directions on what to do during the coming days in the context of FY2014 appropriations negotiations; and providing additional guidance on exceptions to the Antideficiency Act, contracts, grants, information technology, travel, conducting an "orderly shutdown," and payment to excepted employees for time worked).

[34] See U.S. Congress, Senate Committee on the Budget and House Committee on the Budget, Effects of Potential Government Shutdown, hearing, 104th Cong., 1st sess., September 19, 1995, S.Hrg. 104-175 (Washington: GPO, 1995), pp. 77-85; U.S. GAO, Funding Gaps Jeopardize Federal Government Operations, Appendices V, VI, and VII; and U.S. Congress, House Committee on Government Reform and Oversight, Subcommittee on Civil Service, Government Shutdown I: What's Essential? hearings, 104th Cong., 1st sess., December 6 and 14, 1995 (Washington: GPO, 1997), pp. 99-112, 121-131, and 428-430.

[35] See http://www.opm.gov/policy-data-oversight/pay-leave/furlough-guidance/#url=Shutdown-Furlough. This OPM website provides detailed questions and answers about shutdown furloughs in a document titled Guidance for Shutdown Furloughs. The website also explains the distinction between shutdown furloughs and another type of furlough: "administrative furloughs." In brief, the website says a shutdown furlough (also called an emergency furlough) occurs when there is a lapse in appropriations. An affected agency would have to shut down any activities funded by annual appropriations that are not excepted by law. Typically, an agency will have very little to no lead time to plan and implement a shutdown furlough. An administrative furlough, by contrast, is a planned event by an agency which is designed to absorb reductions necessitated by downsizing, reduced funding, lack of work, or any budget situation other than a lapse in appropriations. Furloughs that would potentially result from sequestration would generally be considered administrative furloughs. For more information about sequestration, see CRS Report R42972, Sequestration as a Budget Enforcement Process: Frequently Asked Questions, by Megan S. Lynch.

[36] See OMB Memorandum M-11-13, Planning for Agency Operations During a Lapse in Government Funding, April 7, 2011, p. 16; OMB Memorandum M-12-03, Planning for Agency Operations During a Lapse in Government Funding, December 15, 2011, Attachment 1 (last two pages of non-paginated attachment); and, for the text excerpted above, OMB Memorandum M-13-22, Planning for Agency Operations During a Potential Lapse in Appropriations, September 17, 2013, pp. 15-16.

[37] Various legislative provisions addressed the topic of retroactive salary payment after the FY1996 shutdowns. For instance, a CR provision required that employees who were

furloughed during the first FY1996 shutdown period be paid retroactively (P.L. 104-56, Section 124, 109 Stat. 553, November 20, 1995). In addition, the CR language ratified and approved "[a]ll obligations incurred in anticipation of the appropriations made and authority granted by this Act for the purposes of maintaining the essential level of activity to protect life and property and bring about orderly termination of Government functions." This provision was extended by P.L. 104-94, which applied to the second FY1996 shutdown period (110 Stat. 25, January 6, 1996). Separate legislation explicitly provided FY1996 funding, through January 26, 1996, for salaries of employees who were excepted from furlough and who worked during either of the shutdown periods on projects and activities that were continuing from the previous fiscal year (P.L. 104-92, Section 301, 110 Stat. 19). This legislation also explicitly said all officers and employees of the federal government and the District of Columbia were deemed to be excepted employees from December 15, 1995, through January 26, 1996, during and beyond the second shutdown period (P.L. 104-92, Section 310). It should be noted that affected employees did not receive compensation until funding for their agencies was enacted.

[38] This paragraph was prepared by Jessica Tollestrup, Analyst on Congress and the Legislative Process (jtollestrup@crs.loc.gov, 7-0941) and Clinton T. Brass, Specialist in Government Organization and Management (cbrass@crs.loc.gov, 7-4536) and also draws on CRS Report RS20348, Federal Funding Gaps: A Brief Overview, by Jessica Tollestrup, and CRS Report 95-906, Shutdown of the Federal Government: Effects on the Federal Workforce And Other Sectors, by James P. McGrath (September 25, 1997, out of print; available upon request).

[39] The figure of 800,000 federal employees was frequently cited at the time. For example, see U.S. Congress, House Committee on Government Reform and Oversight, Subcommittee on Civil Service, Government Shutdown I: What's Essential? hearings, 104th Cong., 1st sess., December 6 and 14, 1995 (Washington: GPO, 1997), pp. 6 and 265; and U.S. President (Clinton), The White House, Office of the Press Secretary, "Statement by the President," November 19, 1995, at http://clinton6.nara.gov/1995/11/1995-11-19-president-statement-on-signing-appropriations-bills.html.

[40] H.J.Res. 115. A measure that would have temporarily increased the debt limit, H.R. 2586, also was vetoed on November 13, 1995. As of November 13, three of the 13 regular appropriations acts for FY1996 had been enacted: the Military Construction Appropriations Act (P.L. 104-32), the Agriculture, Rural Development, Food and Drug Administration, and Related Agencies Appropriations Act (P.L. 104-37), and the Energy and Water Development Appropriations Act (P.L. 104-46). Therefore, 10 regular appropriations bills remained unenacted at the start of the first shutdown.

[41] As of December 15, 1995, four additional regular appropriations acts for FY1996 had been enacted: the Department of Transportation and Related Agencies Appropriations Act (P.L. 104-50); the Treasury, Postal Service, and General Government Appropriations Act (P.L. 104-52); the Legislative Branch Appropriations Act (P.L. 104-53); and the Department of Defense Appropriations Act (P.L. 104-61). Therefore, six regular appropriations bills remained unenacted at the start of the second shutdown. These included the (1) Department of Interior and Related Agencies Appropriations Act, (2) Department of Veterans Affairs and Housing and Urban Development, and Independent Agencies Appropriations Act, (3) Department of Commerce and Related Agencies Appropriations Act, (4) Foreign Operations, Export Financing, and Related Programs Appropriations Act, (5) Departments of Labor, Health and Human Services, and Education, and Related Agencies Appropriations Act, and (6) District of Columbia Appropriations Act.

[42] Fewer employees, agencies, and programs were affected, because some funding bills were enacted during and after the first shutdown, and before the second shutdown.

[43] CRS Report RS20348, Federal Funding Gaps: A Brief Overview, by Jessica Tollestrup.

[44] For additional discussion, see U.S. GAO, Principles of Federal Appropriations Law, vol. II, pp. 6-149 - 6-150. According to guidance that OPM issued, individuals appointed by the President (Senate-confirmed and not Senate-confirmed) whose basic pay exceeds the highest rate payable under the General Schedule are not subject to 5 U.S.C. §6301, relating to annual and sick leave, and are not subject to furlough. OPM has explained that "[t]he salary of such a Presidential appointee is an obligation incurred by the year, without consideration of hours of duty required. Thus, the Presidential appointee cannot be placed in a nonduty, nonpay status." See question #16 from PDF version of OPM Web page providing guidance on furloughs, dated February 25, 2011, at http://nhpa.org/docs/LockoutFurloughGuidanceandInformation.pdf. See also OPM's response to Frequently Asked Question #4, in OPM, Guidance for Administrative Furloughs, March 25, 2013, pp. 2-3, at http://www.opm.gov/policy-data-oversight/payleave/furlough-guidance/#url=Administrative-Furlough.

[45] See OPM, Guidance for Shutdown Furloughs, December 2011, p. 2, at http://www.opm.gov/policy-data-oversight/ pay-leave/furlough-guidance/#url=Shutdown-Furlough. OPM refers agencies to DOJ opinions regarding how to determine which employees are designated to be performing excepted or non-excepted functions. These "excepted" employees for purposes of a shutdown should be clearly distinguished from employees whom agencies may designate as "emergency" employees for purposes of weather, natural disaster, power failure, or other events that result in dismissal or closure. The latter category of "emergency" employees may vary substantially across agencies and over time, depending on "each agency's unique mission requirements and/or circumstances." For discussion, see OPM, Washington, DC, Area Dismissal and Closure Procedures, November 2012, pp. 8-9, at http://www.opm.gov/policydata-oversight/pay-leave/reference-materials/handbooks/.

[46] This section was prepared by Ida A. Brudnick, Specialist on the Congress (ibrudnick @crs.loc.gov, 7-6460), and R. Eric Petersen, Specialist in American National Government (epetersen@crs.loc.gov, 7-0643).

[47] P.L. 97-51; 95 Stat. 966; September 11, 1981 (2 U.S.C. §31 note). Additional information regarding compensation for Members of Congress, including actions in the 112th Congress, is available in CRS Report 97-615, Salaries of Members of Congress: Congressional Votes, 1990-2013, by Ida A. Brudnick.

[48] Congressional employing authorities include the following: individual Members of Congress for staff working in personal offices; chairs of individual House, Senate, and joint committees for committee staff; Members who hold leadership positions for staff in their respective leadership offices; and House or Senate officers or officials for staff working in those offices. In April 2011, in the context of deliberations over FY2011 appropriations, the House Committee on House Administration posted related guidance and issued "Dear Colleague" letters. Planning for operations under a lapse of appropriations was also discussed in U.S. Congress, House, First Semiannual Report on the Activities of the Committee on House Administration, 112th Cong., 1st sess., H.Rept. 112-137 (Washington: GPO, 2011), pp. 19-20. For questions regarding congressional and legislative branch operations, see the "Key Policy Staff" table at the end of this report.

[49] For additional discussion, including the status of legislative branch agencies and personnel, see U.S. GAO, Principles of Federal Appropriations Law, vol. II, pp. 6-149 - 6-150, and U.S.

GAO, Letter from James F. Hinchman, GAO General Counsel, to John J. Kominski, Library of Congress General Counsel, B-241911, October 23, 1990, at http://archive.gao.gov/lglp2pdf23/087761.pdf.

[50] This section was prepared by Barry J. McMillion, Analyst on the Federal Judiciary (bmcmillion@crs.loc.gov, 7- 6025); Denis Steven Rutkus, formerly a Specialist on the Federal Judiciary at CRS; and Lorraine H. Tong, formerly an Analyst in American National Government at CRS.

[51] Background information provided to CRS on January 29, 2013, by staff of the Administrative Office of the U.S. Courts.

[52] Ibid.

[53] Ibid.

[54] Ibid.

[55] Ibid.

[56] Ibid.

[57] Article III, Section 1 of the Constitution provides that the Supreme Court's Justices and judges "in such inferior Courts as the Congress may ... establish," shall "receive for their Services, a Compensation, which shall not be diminished during the Continuance in office." In addition to Supreme Court Justices, this constitutional provision applies to judges receiving appointment to the U.S. District Courts, U.S. Circuit Courts of Appeals, and U.S. Court of International Trade.

[58] Background information provided to CRS on September 23, 2011, and January 29, 2013, by staff of the Administrative Office of U.S. Courts.

[59] OMB, "Agency Contingency Plans," at http://www.whitehouse.gov/omb/contingency-plans.

[60] OMB Memorandum M-13-22, Planning for Agency Operations During a Potential Lapse in Appropriations, September 17, 2013, p. 2.

[61] OMB Memorandum M-11-13, Planning for Agency Operations During a Lapse in Government Funding, April 7, 2011, pp. 4-6; and OMB Memorandum M-12-03, Planning for Agency Operations During a Lapse in Government Funding, December 15, 2011, Attachment 1.

[62] OMB Memorandum M-13-22, Planning for Agency Operations During a Potential Lapse in Appropriations, September 17, 2013, Attachment 1.

[63] OMB Memorandum, Agency Operations in the Absence of Appropriations, November 17, 1981.

[64] In 1981, GAO developed a "hypothetical case" of the possible effects of a 30-day government-wide funding gap and shutdown, which the agency characterized as "unthinkable." After the release of the first Civiletti opinion concerning compliance with the Antideficiency Act, GAO characterized the opinion as "fundamentally alter[ing] the environment in which Federal agencies must prepare for a period of expired appropriations." Previously, interpretation of the Antideficiency Act had been much less strict, as noted earlier in this report. The results of GAO's illustrative survey are available in U.S. GAO, Funding Gaps Jeopardize Federal Government Operations, pp. 48-56.

[65] The examples are drawn from more extensive discussion in CRS Report 95-906, Shutdown of the Federal Government: Effects on the Federal Workforce And Other Sectors, by James P. McGrath (out of print; available upon request). Many of the examples come from media accounts during and after the second shutdown and agency accounts in congressional hearings after the first FY1996 shutdown. For more information, see U.S. Congress, House Committee on Government Reform and Oversight, Subcommittee on Civil Service, Government Shutdown I: What's Essential? hearings, 104th Cong., 1st sess., December 6 and 14, 1995 (Washington: GPO, 1997), at http://www.archive.org/details/ government

shutdo00unit. For additional documentation about the effects of past shutdowns, see CRS Report R41759, Past Government Shutdowns: Key Resources, by Jared C. Nagel and Justin Murray.

[66] U.S. Congress, House Committee on Government Reform and Oversight, Subcommittee on Civil Service, Government Shutdown I: What's Essential? hearings, 104th Cong., 1st sess., December 6 and 14, 1995 (Washington: GPO, 1997), p. 23; and Stephen Barr and Frank Swoboda, "Jobless Aid, Toxic Waste Cleanup Halt," Washington Post, January 3, 1996, p. A1.

[67] U.S. Congress, House Committee on Government Reform and Oversight, Subcommittee on Civil Service, Government Shutdown I: What's Essential? hearings, 104th Cong., 1st sess., December 6 and 14, 1995 (Washington: GPO, 1997), pp. 62 and 228, at http://www.archive.org/details/governmentshutdo00unit; and Stephen Barr and David Montgomery, "At Uncle Sam's No One Answers," Washington Post, November 16, 1995, p. A1.

[68] Dan Morgan and Stephen Barr, "When Shutdown Hits Home Ports," Washington Post, January 8, 1996, p. A1.

[69] Thomas W. Lippman, "Inconvenience Edges Toward Emergency," Washington Post, January 3, 1996, p. A11.

[70] U.S. Congress, House Committee on Government Reform and Oversight, Subcommittee on Civil Service, Government Shutdown I: What's Essential? hearings, 104th Cong., 1st sess., December 6 and 14, 1995 (Washington: GPO, 1997), pp. 115-117.

[71] Peter Behr, "Contractors Face Mounting Costs from Government Shutdowns," Washington Post, January 23, 1996, p. C1; U.S. Congress, House Committee on Government Reform and Oversight, Subcommittee on Civil Service, Government Shutdown I: What's Essential? hearings, 104th Cong., 1st sess., December 6 and 14, 1995 (Washington: GPO, 1997), p. 270, at http://www.archive.org/details/governmentshutdo00unit; and Peter Behr, "Latest Federal Shutdown Hits Contractors Hard," Washington Post, December 22, 1995, p. D1.

[72] See U.S. Congress, House Committee on Government Reform and Oversight, Subcommittee on Civil Service, Government Shutdown I: What's Essential? hearings, 104th Cong., 1st sess., December 6 and 14, 1995 (Washington: GPO, 1997), pp. 266-270 (letter, list of effects, and cost estimate); pp. 272 and 274 (list of agencies and estimates of employees to be excepted or not excepted as of November 15, 1995, apparently corresponding to the first shutdown); and p. 273 (list of agencies and estimates of employees to be excepted or not excepted, in a document dated February 2, 1996, and apparently corresponding to the second shutdown), at http://www.archive.org/details/ governmentshutdo00unit. The list provided on pages 272 and 274 includes agencies that already had received full-year appropriations and therefore may not represent a full accounting of actual furloughs. According to OMB, a portion of shutdown-related costs corresponded to pay for furloughed employees, and additional costs were anticipated from backlogs of work (ibid., p. 226). With regard to costs, President Clinton said that total costs for the two shutdowns amounted to "a billion-and-a-half dollars." See U.S. President (Clinton), The White House, Office of the Press Secretary, "Radio Address by the President to the Nation," press release, January 20, 1996, at http://clinton6.nara.gov/ 1996/01/1996-01-20-presidents-weekly-radio-address-regarding-budget.html.

[73] This paragraph was prepared by Barry J. McMillion, Analyst on the Federal Judiciary (bmcmillion@crs.loc.gov, 7- 6025); Denis Steven Rutkus, formerly a Specialist on the Federal Judiciary at CRS; and Lorraine H. Tong, formerly an Analyst in American National Government at CRS.

[74] See "An Inside Look at the Shutdown," The Third Branch: Newsletter of the Federal Courts, Washington, DC, December 1995, at http://www.uscourts.gov/News/TheThirdBranch/95-12-01/ An_Inside_Look_At_the_Shutdown.aspx; also, "Active, Long, and Contentious First Session of Congress Closes," The Third Branch, Washington, DC, February 1996, at http://www.uscourts.gov/News/TheThirdBranch/96-02-01/ Active_Long_and_Contentious_First_Session_of_Congress_Closes.aspx.

[75] The judiciary also uses non-appropriated funds to offset its appropriations requirement. The majority of these non-appropriated funds are from fee collections, primarily from court filing fees. These monies are used to offset expenses within the Salaries and Expenses account. In some instances, the judiciary also has funds which may carry forward from one year to the next. These funds are considered "unencumbered," because they result from savings from the judiciary's financial plan in areas where budgeted costs did not materialize. According to the judiciary's budget submission to Congress, such savings are usually not under its control (e.g., the judiciary has no control over the confirmation rate of Article III judges and must make its best estimate on the needed funds to budget for judgeships, new rent costs, and technology funding for certain programs).

[76] "An Inside Look at the Shutdown," The Third Branch, Washington, DC, December 1995, at http://www.uscourts.gov/News/TheThirdBranch/95-12-01/An_Inside_Look_At_the_ Shutdown.aspx.

[77] Ibid.

[78] Background information provided to CRS on April 7, 2011, by staff of Administrative Office of the U.S. Courts.

[79] See this report's earlier discussion of the "authorized by law" exceptions to the Antideficiency Act and the 1981 Civiletti opinion, reprinted in U.S. GAO, Funding Gaps Jeopardize Federal Government Operations, p. 82 (footnote 7). For further discussion, see U.S. GAO, Principles of Federal Appropriations Law, vol. II, pp. 6-149 - 6-150.

[80] See SSA's "History of SSA 1993 - 2000," chapter 5, at http://www.ssa.gov/history/ssa/ ssa2000chapter5.html.

[81] This discussion of judiciary operations was prepared by Barry J. McMillion, Analyst on the Federal Judiciary (bmcmillion@crs.loc.gov, 7-6025); Denis Steven Rutkus, formerly a Specialist on the Federal Judiciary at CRS; and Lorraine H. Tong, formerly an Analyst in American National Government at CRS. For additional information related to the Judiciary's contingency planning for a government shutdown during FY2011, see CRS Congressional Distribution Memorandum, Government Shutdown: Possible Effects on Federal Judiciary Operations, by D. Steven Rutkus and Lorraine H. Tong, April 8, 2011 (available from Barry J. McMillion at bmcmillion@crs.loc.govmailto:).

[82] U.S. Administrative Office of the U.S. Courts, "What Happens to Courts if the Federal Government Closes?" press release, April 5, 2011, at http://www.uscourts.gov/News/ NewsView/11-04-05/ What_Happens_to_Courts_if_the_Federal_Government_Closes.aspx.

[83] Ibid.

[84] Background information provided to CRS on April 7, 2011, by staff of Administrative Office of the U.S. Courts.

[85] The plans were posted online, at OMB, "Agency Contingency Plans," at http://www. whitehouse.gov/omb/ contingency-plans.

[86] OMB Memorandum M-13-22, Planning for Agency Operations During a Potential Lapse in Appropriations, September 17, 2013, Attachment 1.

[87] CRS Report R42469, Government Procurement in Times of Fiscal Uncertainty, by Kate M. Manuel and Erika K. Lunder.

[88] CRS Report R41745, Government Shutdown: Operations of the Department of Defense During a Lapse in Appropriations, by Pat Towell and Amy Belasco.

[89] See U.S. Congress, House Committee on Government Reform and Oversight, Subcommittee on Civil Service, Government Shutdown I: What's Essential? hearings, 104th Cong., 1st sess., December 6 and 14, 1995 (Washington: GPO, 1997), pp. 1-3.

[90] Ibid., p. 2.

[91] Ibid.

[92] OMB, Circular No. A-11: Preparation, Submission, and Execution of the Budget, August 2012, Section 124, p. 1.

[93] Ibid., pp. 1-2.

[94] This section was prepared by John Rollins, Specialist in Terrorism and National Security (jrollins@crs.loc.gov, 7- 5529).

[95] While an incident of national security significance could entail actions undertaken by a group of individuals, response and recovery efforts associated with a catastrophic natural disaster also may be an issue of concern.

[96] For information and analysis related to possible security vulnerabilities during periods of government uncertainty, see CRS Report R42773, 2012-2013 Presidential Election Period: National Security Considerations and Options, by John W. Rollins.

[97] For example, see OMB Memorandum, Agency Operations in the Absence of Appropriations, November 17, 1981. See also U.S. Department of Defense, Guidance for Continuation of Operations in the Absence of Available Appropriations, April 7, 2011, at http://www.defense.gov/home/features/2011/0411_govtshutdown/OSD_04092- 11.pdf.

[98] Responsibility for overseeing the nation's security interests are shared by organizations within the intelligence, law enforcement, and national and homeland security communities. For discussion of the effect of a government shutdown on Department of Defense related activities, see CRS Report R41745, Government Shutdown: Operations of the Department of Defense During a Lapse in Appropriations, by Pat Towell and Amy Belasco.

In: The Government Shutdown of 2013 ISBN: 978-1-63117-112-3
Editor: Rosanne C. Lundy © 2014 Nova Science Publishers, Inc.

Chapter 2

ECONOMIC ACTIVITY DURING THE GOVERNMENT SHUTDOWN AND DEBT LIMIT BRINKSMANSHIP[*]

Council of Economic Advisers

INTRODUCTION

The government shutdown and debt limit brinksmanship have had a substantial negative impact on the economy. The shutdown directly affected the economy by withdrawing government services for a sixteen day period, which not only had direct impacts but also had a range of indirect effects on the private sector. For example the travel industry was hurt by the closing of national parks, businesses in oil and gas and other industries were hurt by the cessation of permits for oil and gas drilling, the housing industry was hurt by the cessation of IRS verifications for mortgage applications, and small businesses were hurt by the shutdown of Small Business Administration loan guarantees. In addition, a reduction in consumer confidence and an increase in uncertainty associated not just with the shutdown but also the brinksmanship over the debt limit affected consumer spending, investment and hiring as well.

A number of private sector analyses have estimated that the shutdown reduced the annualized growth rate of GDP in the fourth quarter by anywhere

---

[*] This is an edited, reformatted and augmented version of a Council of Economic Advisers publication, dated October 2013.

from 0.2 percentage point (as estimated by JP Morgan) to 0.6 percentage point (as estimated by Standard and Poor's), with intermediate estimates of 0.2 percentage point and 0.5 percentage point from Macroeconomic Advisers and Goldman Sachs respectively. Most of the private sector analyses are based on models that predict the impact of the shutdown based on the reduction in government services over that period. Very few of them are based on an actual analysis of economic performance during the period of the shutdown and very few take into account the secondary effects on the private sector of the cessation of government services or the effects on confidence and uncertainty associated with both the shutdown and the debt limit brinksmanship. But we know that these effects can be large; for example, the debt limit brinksmanship in the summer of 2011 had an adverse economic impact even though it was not accompanied by a shutdown nor did it lead to an actual default on U.S. government obligations. While useful in understanding the costs of the shutdown and brinksmanship, the available private-sector analyses present only part of the picture.

This report attempts to estimate the actual impact of the shutdown and default brinksmanship on economic activity as measured by eight different daily or weekly economic indicators. *Overall it finds that a range of eight economic indicators combined in what this report calls a "Weekly Economic Index" are consistent with a 0.25 percentage point reduction in the annualized GDP growth rate in the fourth quarter and a reduction of about 120,000 private-sector jobs in the first two weeks of October (estimates use indicators available through October 12th.)*

These estimates could understate the full economic effects of the episode to the degree it continues to have an effect past October 12th.

SUMMARY OF ECONOMIC DATA FOR THE FIRST HALF OF OCTOBER AND THE WEEKLY ECONOMIC INDEX

The attempt to create an immediate estimate of economic impact is frustrated by the fact that most economic data are reported with a long lag (for example, most October data will be released in mid-to-late November), are reported on a monthly rather than a weekly basis and the weekly and daily data have substantial volatility. These limitations were compounded during the shutdown as virtually all government data, with the exception of weekly unemployment insurance claims, were halted. By combining a range of indictors that are individually noisy it is possible to gather evidence about the trajectory of the economy over shorter periods, including during the first half of October.

Such short windows are often uninteresting given the noise in the data and the generally slow shifts in major economic trends. However, during periods with a sharp break in the economic environment—like the recent shutdown and debt limit brinksmanship—such estimates can provide a valuable clue to the direction of the economy.

Table 1 shows eight different measures of economic performance and sentiment in the first half of October. All eight indicators deteriorate in the first half of October, with the contractions being very sharp in several cases.

Table 1. Weekly Economic Indicators and Index, October 2013

	Week ending 9/28	Week ending 10/12	Change
Johnson-Redbook Same-Store Sales Index (y/y % chge)	3.8	3.2	-0.6
ICSC Same-Store Sales Index (y/y % chge)	2.1	1.0	-1.1
New UI Claims (thousands)	308	358	50
Gallup Job Creation Index	19.7	16.8	-2.8
Gallup Economic Confidence Index	-21.5	-38.2	-16.7
Rasmussen Consumer Index	99.9	91.8	-8.1
AISI Raw Steel Production (y/y % chge)	4.0	6.2	2.2
MBA Mortgage Applications (y/y % chge)	-2.5	-11.5	-9.0
Weekly Economic Index	3.6	2.0	-1.6

To understand what this means for overall economic activity CEA combined these indicators into a "Weekly Economic Index" that is scaled to match the overall growth rate of economic activity (see Figure 1). This "Weekly Economic Index" is designed to extract the main common "signal" from the noise of these different indicators. As discussed in more detail later in this Report, this Weekly Economic Index was designed to estimate the co-movements among these eight indicators, not to predict any particular monthly data series.

Nevertheless, the Weekly Economic Index turns out to be highly correlated with standard monthly measures of economic activity, notably changes in employment and the growth of industrial production.

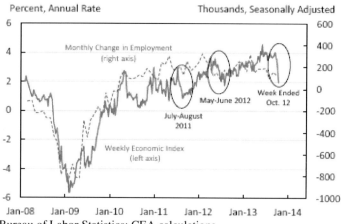

Source: Bureau of Labor Statistics; CEA calculations.

Figure 1. WeeklyEconomic Index and Monthly Change in Private Employment.

This Weekly Economic Index is calibrated to be consistent with the magnitudes of growth rates in GDP and shows a sharp 1.6 percentage point reduction in the economic growth rate in the fourth quarter if it were sustained for the full 13 weeks of the fourth quarter. Our focus is on the first two weeks of October, and these data suggests that the decline over this period will reduce the GDP growth rate by 0.25 percentage point at an annual rate (about two-thirteenths of the reduction in the index reflecting the two weeks we are analyzing). When calibrated to employment growth the Index suggests 120,000 fewer private-sector jobs were created in the first two weeks of October than would have been created without the shutdown and debt limit brinksmanship.

THE WEEKLY DATA SERIES

The eight series used to construct the index include two measures of retail sales, two measures of consumer confidence, two measures of labor market activity, one measure of production, and one measure of housing market activity. The series, their source, and release dates relative to the observation][period are listed in Table 2. Seven of the series are privately produced and are based on privately-reported data, while one series, new claims for unemployment insurance (UI), is produced by the Department of Labor. All these series were released during the shutdown. Three of the series – the

Gallup Economic Confidence Index, the Rasmussen Consumer Index, and the Gallup Job Creation Index – are available daily, while the rest are reported weekly.[1]

Table 2. Description of Variables

Series Name	Frequency	Release Date	Source
Consumer Spending			
ICSC Same-Store Retail Sales (52-week growth, %)	Weekly	Following Tuesday	International Council of Shopping Centers
Redbook Same-Store Retail Sales (y/y growth, %)	Weekly	Following Tuesday	Johnson Redbook Service
Consumer Confidence			
Gallup Economic Confidence	Daily	Next day	Gallup
Rasmussen Consumer Index	Daily	Same day	Rasmussen Reports
Labor Market			
Gallup Job Creation Index	Daily	Next day	Gallup
Unemployment Insurance (Initial Claims)	Weekly	Following Thursday	Department of Labor
Industrial Production			
Raw Steel Production (52-week growth, %)	Weekly	Following Monday	American Iron and Steel Institute
Housing Market			
Mortgage Purchase Applications (52-week growth, %)	Weekly	Following Wednesday	Mortgage Bankers Association

The eight indicators are plotted in Figures 2-5. Figure 2 shows the two retail sales indexes, one constructed by the International Council of Shopping Centers (ICSC) the other by Johnson Redbook Service. These series measure the growth in same-store sales over the past 52 weeks. Both series are noisy partly because the sample of stores is small and because sales fluctuate considerably depending on dates of holidays and major weather systems. Figure 2 also shows the 12-month growth in monthly Real Retail Sales and Food Services, a measure of sales that includes a wider segment of the retail sector and is based on a larger sample. Although the two weekly series have a long-term trend similar to that of the monthly sales series, at any given date the two weekly series diverge from the Census series and from each other. Recently, the Redbook series has shown stronger sales growth than the ICSC series.

Figure 2.

The two labor market variables, shown in Figure 3, are weekly initial claims for unemployment insurance and the daily Gallup Job Creation Index. The Gallup Job Creation Index is based on a daily random digit dial telephone survey that asks respondents whether their employer is increasing or reducing employment (the job creation index is presented here on an inverted scale to make it easier to compare with unemployment insurance claims). These two series track each other closely and share many common features, including the spike in the week ending October 5.

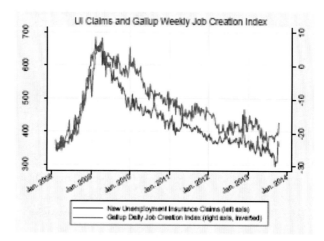

Figure 3.

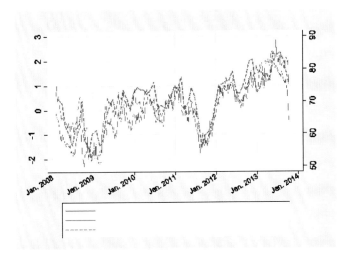

Figure 4.

Figure 4 shows the two daily confidence measures, the daily Gallup Economic Confidence Index and daily Rasmussen Consumer Index, which are plotted on a standardized scale to simplify comparison. The two daily indexes track each other and also track the monthly University of Michigan Index of Consumer Sentiment. The three confidence measures are based on independent surveys and use differently worded questions. All three measures show a sharp decline in the first two weeks of October.

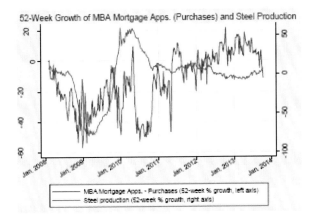

Figure 5.

Figures 5 shows the 52-week growth in the Mortgage Bankers' Association weekly mortgage applications for new purchases and the 52-week growth in the American Iron and Steel Institute's raw steel production series. Although both series slumped sharply during the recession, they show different patterns during the recovery: weekly steel production grew quickly early in the recovery, then slowed, whereas the mortgage applications for new purchases started to recover only later, both because of the delayed recovery of the housing market and because of the relatively large fraction of cash purchases early in the recovery.

CONSTRUCTION OF THE WEEKLY ECONOMIC INDEX

As can be seen in Figures 2-5, these weekly series exhibit considerable noise from week to week, so that gleaning broader trends from any one series is difficult. They also, however, display a clear cyclical pattern, which suggests that these series might usefully be combined into a single index. The Weekly Economic Index is computed from these eight series using the method of principal component analysis. The principal component of these eight series provides an estimate of a signal about the economy which is common to all eight. The mathematics of principal components analysis is summarized in the Appendix.

The resulting Weekly Economic Index is shown in Figure 1. By construction, the Weekly Economic Index is a weighted average of the eight series. The weekly index explains 58% of the overall variance of the eight component series. The Weekly Economic Index is a measure of economic growth, and for ease of interpretation it has been scaled to have the same mean as the four-quarter growth in real GDP from 2008 to the present. The units of the Weekly Index are therefore the units of GDP growth at an annual rate.[2]

RELATIONSHIP OF THE WEEKLY INDEX TO MONTHLY EMPLOYMENT AND INDUSTRIAL PRODUCTION

The weekly index is designed to be a gauge of overall economic activity in the current week and is not intended to forecast the growth of any specific major economic indicator. Nevertheless, as seen in Figure 6, the index tracks the overall pattern of changes in monthly private and total employment. When the weekly index is aggregated to the monthly level, the correlation between the index and the monthly change in total employment is 0.86 (0.87 excluding Census workers), and the correlation between the index and the monthly change in private employment is 0.87.

Figure 6.

The weekly index also tracks other major economic indicators. The correlation between the index and the twelve-month growth of the Index of Industrial Production is 0.84, and its correlation with the twelve-month growth of real manufacturing and trade sales is 0.86.

REGRESSION RESULTS AND SENSITIVITY CHECKS

Figure 6 indicates that the Weekly Economic Index moves together with changes in monthly employment. This co-movement can be summarized in a regression of the changes of monthly employment on monthly values of the index, and the results of this regression are shown in Table 3 for monthly changes in private payroll employment. For the Weekly Economic Index, the adjusted R^2 of this regression is 75%.

We computed a number of other indexes as sensitivity checks. Two of these indexes are computed as the principal component of a subset of the eight variables: the 6-variable index drops steel production and MBA mortgage applications, and the 5-variable index also drops UI claims. An alternative 6-variable index was also computed using state space methods, with the index estimated using the Kalman filter as discussed in the appendix. Regressions relating changes in private employment to these three additional indexes are reported in Table 3.

The regressions confirm that the three indexes have very similar predictive content for monthly changes in private employment, and the results for total employment (not shown) are similar to those in Table 3.

Table 3. Monthly Aggregate of the Weekly Index and Private Employment: Regression Results
Sample: monthly, February 2008 – August 2013 Dependent variable: Change in Private Employment

Regressors	(1)	(2)	(3)	(4)
	115**			
Weekly Economic Index	(8)			
Sensitivity checks:				
		114**		
5-variable index		(8)		
			111**	
6-variable index			(9)	
6-variable index estimated by the				120**
Kalman Filter				(8)
Adjusted R2	0.75	0.74	0.72	0.77
Standard Error of the Regression	154	157	164	147

Notes: Each column summarizes the results of a regression of monthly change in private payroll employment on a weekly index, where the weekly index is aggregated to monthly (data for a week overlapping two months are assigned proportionately to the two months). Entries are regression coefficients, with heteroskedasticity- and autocorrelation-robust standard errors in parentheses. The sample size is shorter for the regressions involving the 9-indicator index because that index is available starting February 2009. Coefficients are statistically significant at the +10%, *5%, **10% significance level.

Table 3 answers, in the affirmative, the question of whether the index is correlated with changes in employment. A separate question is whether the index contains information useful for predicting monthly changes in employment going forward, beyond the information contained in past values of changes of employment. This question is examined in Table 4. The regressions in Table 4 take advantage of the weekly nature of index and use values of the index for the four weeks between the two measurement reference weeks for payroll employment. Broadly speaking, the Establishment Survey aims to estimate payroll employment on the 12th day of the month. The weekly data structure permits estimation of the effect of economic developments between these reference dates from one month to the next. Accordingly, in these regressions, payroll employment in a given month is predicted using data for the first two seven-day periods of the month, the third seven-day period of the previous month, and the final seven-to-ten day period of the previous month – that is, the weeks between the Establishment Survey reference date – along with changes of payroll employment from the previous month.

Two findings in Table 4 are noteworthy. First, the test of the hypothesis that the coefficients on the four weekly values of the index are zero constitutes a test of marginal predictive content (a so-called Granger Causality test). For the Weekly Index and the four sensitivity check indexes, this hypothesis is rejected at the 5% significance level, indicating that the indexes help to forecast employment changes beyond the lagged value of employment. Second, the hypothesis that the coefficients on the four weeks are equal is rejected for all the indexes; instead of equality, the coefficients show a similar pattern across indexes in which the change in the index between the last two weeks of the previous month and the first two weeks of the current month is a useful predictor of employment. Because these regressions contain lagged changes in employment, this pattern is consistent with the interpretation of this regression as estimating changes in employment, relative to the previous month.

The final line of Table 4 reports estimates of the change in private employment arising from the shutdown. These estimates were computed by comparing the actual value of the index for the first two weeks of October to the counterfactual in which those values for the first two weeks of October were the same as for the last week in September. The estimate based on the Weekly Economic Index is a reduction in job changes in October – the immediate cost of the shutdown, measured in terms of jobs – is 120 thousand jobs lost. The estimates based on the other indexes range between 106 -128 thousand jobs lost.

Table 4. Weekly Values of the Index as a Predictor of Changes in Employment Sample: monthly, February 2008 – August 2013

Regressors	(1) Weekly Economic Index	(2) 5-variable index	(3) 6-variable index	(4) 6-variable index, Kalman Filter
Current month, week 2	81.1	56.5	62.1	75.3
	(33.7)	(28.2)	(34.1)	(48.0)
Current month, week 1	4.9	28.1	28.6	41.6
	(48.9)	(37.8)	(46.9)	(67.4)
Last month, week 4	-17.4	-56.7	-41.3	-118.6
	(50.9)	(35.7)	(45.5)	(59.6)
Last month, week 3	-65.6	-20.6	-48.5	6.9
	(42.0)	(31.9)	(40.6)	(45.0)
first lag of change in empl.	0.61	0.62	0.65	0.61
	(0.12)	(0.12)	(0.12)	(0.12)
second lag of change in empl.	0.30	0.27	0.29	0.30
	(0.13)	(0.12)	(0.13)	(0.13)
F-test of that coefficients on all four weekly variables = 0	3.82	3.96	3.72	3.27
	(0.01)	(0.01)	(0.01)	(0.02)
F-test of equality of coefficients on all four weekly variables	4.99	5.27	4.77	4.21
	(0.00)	(0.00)	(0.00)	(0.01)
Adjusted R2	0.90	0.90	0.90	0.89
Standard Error of the Regression	99	99	99	100
Predicted Change in Total Employment (Thousands)	-120	-126	-128	-106

Notes: Each column summarizes the results of a regression of monthly change in private employment on weekly values of an index, where the first three weekly values in a month correspond to the first through third 7-day period of the month and final weekly value corresponds to the final 7-10 day period, where data for calendar weeks overlapping adjacent 7- day periods are assigned to the two periods proportionately. Entries in the top panel are regression coefficients, with standard errors in parentheses, and in the lower panel are F-statistics with p-values in parentheses. The sample size is shorter for the regressions involving the 9-indicator index because that index is available starting February 2009. Coefficients are statistically significant at the +10%, *5%, **10% significance level.

CONCLUSION

In normal times estimating weekly changes in the economy is likely to detract from the focus on the more meaningful longer term trends in the economy which are best measured over a monthly, quarterly, or even yearly basis. But when there is a sharp shift in the economic environment, analyzing high-frequency changes with only a very short lag since they occurred can be very valuable. This paper shows that a range of indicators show that sentiment, job creation, consumption, and some elements of production grew more slowly in the first half of October than in previous months. Moreover, it combines all of these indicators into a single measure termed the Weekly Economic Index which is consistent with a 0.25 percentage point reduction in the annualized GDP growth rate in the fourth quarter or a reduction of about 120 thousand jobs in October, based solely on the indicators available covering the period through October 12th. These estimates could understate the full economic effects of the episode to the degree it continues to have an effect past October 12th—as it most likely would. This is just a first attempt to analyze these data and as updated data and further research becomes available it could lead to refinements in these estimates.

APPENDIX: PRINCIPAL COMPONENTS ESTIMATION OF DYNAMIC FACTOR MODELS

A leading framework for the construction of an economic index from multiple time series is the so-called dynamic factor model, developed by Geweke (1977). The dynamic factor model posits the existence of a small number of unobserved or latent series, called factors, which drive the co-movements of the observed economic time series. Application of dynamic factor models to estimating economic indexes range from the construction of state-level indexes of economic activity (Crone and Clayton-Matthews (2005)) to large-scale indexes of economic activity (for example, the Chicago Fed National Activity Index, or CFNAI). Stock and Watson (2011) provide a review of the econometric theory of dynamic factor models, including recent applications.

The premise of a dynamic factor model is that a small number – in the application of this Report, a single – latent factor, f_t, drives the co-movements of a vector of N time-series variables, X_t. The dynamic factor model posits that the observed series is the sum of the dynamic effect of the common factor and an idiosyncratic disturbance, e_t, which arise from measurement error and from special features that are specific to an individual series:

$$X_t = \lambda_t(L) f_t + e_t \qquad (1)$$

where L is the lag operator. The elements of the $N \times 1$ vector of lag polynomials $f_i(L)$ are the dynamic factor loadings, and $\lambda_{ti}(L) f_t$ is called the common component of the ith series. The dynamic factor can be rewritten in static form by stacking f_t and its lags into single vector F_t, which has dimension up to the number of lags in $)_t(L)$:

$$X_t = AF_t + e_t \qquad (2)$$

where A is a matrix with rows being the coefficients in the lag polynomial $\lambda(L)$.

The two primary methods for estimating the unobserved factor f_t are by principal components and using state space methods, where the factor is estimated by the Kalman filter. Broadly speaking, early low-dimensional applications used parametric state-space methods and more recent high-dimensional applications tend to use nonparametric principal components or variants. The key theoretical result justifying the use of principal components is that the principal components estimator of the factor (or, more generally, the space spanned by the factors) s is consistent and moreover, if N is sufficiently large, then the factors are estimated precisely enough to be treated as data in subsequent regressions.

The principal components estimator of F_t is the weighted average $\hat{\Lambda}' X_t$, where $\hat{\Lambda}$ is the matrix of eigenvectors of the sample variance matrix of X_t, $\hat{\Sigma}_x =$ $1 / T_{tt} T X X_{=}' \Sigma$, associated with the r largest eigenvalues of $\hat{\Sigma}_x$, where here r=1. The principal components estimator can be derived as the solution to the least squares problem,

$$\min_{F_1,\ldots,F_T,\Lambda} V_r(\Lambda, F), \text{ where } V_r(\Lambda, F) = \frac{1}{NT} \sum_{t=1}^{T} (X_t - \Lambda F_t)'(X_t - \Lambda F_t), \qquad (3)$$

subject to the normalization $N_{-1}\Lambda'\Lambda = I_r$. Consistency of the principal components estimator of F_t was first shown for T fixed and $N \to \infty$ in the exact static factor model by Connor and Korajczyk (1986). Stock and Watson (2002a) proved uniform consistency of the factors under weaker conditions along the lines of Chamberlain and Rothschild's (1983) approximate factor model, allowing for weak serial and cross-correlation in the idiosyncratic errors. Stock and Watson (2002a) also provided rate conditions on N and T under which $\hat{}_t F$ can be treated as data for the purposes of a second stage least squares regression (that is, in which the estimation error in $\hat{}_t F$ does not affect the asymptotic distribution of the OLS coefficients with $\hat{}_t F$ as a regressor). Bai (2003) provides limiting distributions for the estimated factors and common components Bai and Ng (2006a) provide improved rates, specifically $N \to \infty$, $T \to \infty$, and $N_2/T \to \infty$, under which $\hat{}_t F$ is consistent and can be treated as data in subsequent regressions; they also provide results for construction of confidence intervals for common components estimated using $\hat{}_t F$.

The main alternative estimation method is to specify a parametric factor model, to estimate the parameters by maximum likelihood, and to estimate the factor using the Kalman filter; for initial applications of this approach see Engle and Watson (1981), Sargent (1989), and Stock and Watson (1989, 1991). In practice the resulting estimates can be sensitive to the parametric specification of the model, so principal components estimation is used in this Report. As a sensitivity check, however, we also considered the six-variable index estimated using the Kalman filter. Regression results for that index are similar to those reported in Tables 3 and 4. An alternative approach to using high-frequency data for real-time monitoring ("nowcasting") is to focus on forecasting a specific economic release, such as the monthly change in employment, and to construct a model that updates those forecasts as new data comes in. The dynamic factor model and its state space implementation is useful for this purpose because a single model automatically adapts to new data becoming available to estimate the variable of interest. For applications of dynamic factor models to nowcasting, see Giannone, Reichlin and Small (2008) and Aruoba, Diebold and Scotti (2009).

REFERENCES

Aruoba, S.B., F.X. Diebold, and C. Scotti, (2009), "Real-Time Measurement of Business Conditions," *Journal of Business & Economic Statistics* 27, 417-427.

Bai, J., (2003), "Inferential Theory for Factor Models of Large Dimensions," *Econometrica*, 71, 135-172.

Bai, J., and S. Ng, (2006), "Confidence Intervals for Diffusion Index Forecasts and Inference for Factor-Augmented Regressions," *Econometrica*, 74,1133-1150.

Chamberlain, G., and M. Rothschild, (1983), "Arbitrage Factor Structure, and Mean-Variance Analysis of Large Asset Markets," *Econometrica*, 51,1281-1304.

Crone, T.S. and A Clayton-Matthews, (2005), "Consistent Economic Estimates for the 50 States," *The Review of Economics and Statistics*, 87, 593-603.

Engle, R.F., and M.W. Watson, (1981), "A One-Factor Multivariate Time Series Model of Metropolitan Wage Rates," *Journal of the American Statistical Association*, 76, 774-781.

Geweke, J., (1977), "The Dynamic Factor Analysis of Economic Time Series," in *Latent Variables in Socio-Economic Models*, ed. by D.J. Aigner and A.S. Goldberger, Amsterdam: North-Holland.

Giannone, D., L. Reichlin, and D. Small, (2008), "Nowcasting: The Real-Time Informational Content of Macroeconomic Data," *Journal of Monetary Economics*, 55, 665-676.

Sargent, T.J., (1989), "Two Models of Measurements and the Investment Accelerator," *Journal of Political Economy* 97:251–287.

Stock, J.H., and M.W. Watson, (1989), "New Indexes of Coincident and Leading Economic Indicators," *NBER Macroeconomics Annual 1989*, 351-393.

Stock, J.H., and M.W. Watson, (1999), "Forecasting Inflation," *Journal of Monetary Economics*, 44, 293-335.

Stock, J.H., and M.W. Watson, (2002), "Forecasting Using Principal Components from a Large Number of Predictors," *Journal of the American Statistical Association*, 97, 1167-1179.

Stock, J.H., and M.W. Watson, (2011), "Dynamic Factor Models," ch. 2 in M. Clements and D. Hendry (eds.), *Oxford Handbook of Economic Forecasting*. Oxford: Oxford University Press.

In: The Government Shutdown of 2013
Editor: Rosanne C. Lundy

ISBN: 978-1-63117-112-3
© 2014 Nova Science Publishers, Inc.

Chapter 3

IMPACTS AND COSTS OF THE OCTOBER 2013 FEDERAL GOVERNMENT SHUTDOWN[*]

*Office of Management and Budget,
Executive Office of the President
of the United States*

EXECUTIVE SUMMARY

The October 2013 Federal government shutdown was the second longest since 1980 and the most significant on record, measured in terms of employee furlough days. Outside experts estimate that the shutdown will reduce fourth quarter Gross Domestic Product (GDP) growth by 0.2-0.6 percentage points. The Council of Economic Advisers estimates that the combination of the government shutdown and debt limit brinksmanship may have resulted in 120,000 fewer private-sector jobs created during the first two weeks of October.[1]

This report examines the economic, budgetary, and programmatic costs of the government shutdown. These costs include economic disruption, Federal employee furloughs, programmatic impacts, other costs to the Federal budget, and impacts on the Federal workforce.

---

[*] This is an edited, reformatted and augmented version of Office of Management and Budget, Executive Office of the President of the United States publication, dated November 2013.

Economic Disruption

Independent forecasters estimate that the shutdown will lower fourth quarter real GDP growth by 0.2-0.6 percentage points, or $2-$6 billion in lost output. Most of these estimates of the shutdown's economic costs are model-based projections, which incorporate only the shutdown's effects on the flow of government spending. As a result, they may not fully account for the direct economic disruption that resulted from the shutdown of government services important to the functioning of the private economy.

The Federal government shutdown:

- *Halted permitting and environmental and other reviews, delaying job-creating transportation and energy projects.* For example, *the Bureau of Land Management (BLM) was unable to process about 200 Applications for Permit to Drill,* delaying energy development on Federal lands in North Dakota, Wyoming, Utah, and other states.
- *Hindered trade by putting import and export licenses and applications on hold.* For example, because the Treasury Department's Alcohol and Tobacco Tax and Trade Bureau was unable to issue export certificates for beer, wine, and distilled spirits, *more than two million liters of U.S. products were left sitting at ports unable to ship.*
- *Disrupted private-sector lending to individuals and small businesses.* During the shutdown, banks and other lenders could not access government income and Social Security Number verification services. Two weeks into the shutdown, *the Internal Revenue Service (IRS) had an inventory of 1.2 million verification requests that could not be processed,* potentially delaying approval of mortgages and other loans.
- *Halted Federal loans to small businesses, homeowners, and housing and healthcare facility developers. The Small Business Administration (SBA) was unable to process about 700 applications for $140 million in small business loans,* and *the Federal Housing Administration (FHA) was unable to process over 500 applications for loans to develop, rehabilitate, or refinance around 80,000 multifamily rental units.*
- *Delayed the Alaskan crab fishing season, costing fisherman thousands of dollars in lost revenue.* Because the National Oceanic and Atmospheric Administration (NOAA) was unable to apportion harvest levels, the start of the season was delayed for three to four days. *The*

fishing industry estimates these delays cost fisherman thousands of dollars of lost revenue per day, since days lost at the beginning of the season cannot be made up later.
- *Disrupted tourism and travel by closing national parks and the Smithsonian.* The National Park Service (NPS) estimates that *the shutdown led to over $500 million in lost visitor spending nationwide*, a significant economic hit to communities surrounding national parks and monuments.
- *Significantly impacted small businesses that contract with the Federal government.* Compared with the same period last year, *small business contracts with the Department of Defense (DOD) dropped by almost one-third during the shutdown, and spending dropped 40 percent.*
- *Delayed aircraft purchases and deliveries by closing the Federal Aviation Administration (FAA)'s Aircraft Registry.* The General Aviation Manufacturers Association estimates that this delayed *156 aircraft deliveries valued at $1.9 billion.*
- *Delayed Food and Drug Administration (FDA) approval of medical products, devices, and drugs.* This delayed businesses in moving products to market.
- *Deprived businesses of important information about the state of the economy.* During the shutdown, Federal statistical agencies were unable to release data and reports ranging from the October jobs report and the Consumer Price Index to the Energy Information Administration's reports on petroleum, diesel prices, heating oil, and natural gas storage. Businesses count on these data to make investment, pricing, and other decisions.

Federal Employee Furloughs

During the 16-day shutdown, *Federal government employees were furloughed for a combined total of 6.6 million days*, more than during any previous Federal government shutdown. Employees not on the job could not conduct food, product, and workplace safety inspections; prepare for flu season or monitor other public health issues; process tax refunds or respond to taxpayer questions; or provide numerous other services important to the general public and the economy.

One way to quantify the cost of Federal employee furloughs is in terms of payroll costs for furloughed employee pay --- costs the Federal government incurred for services that could not be performed. We estimate that *the total cost of pay for furloughed Federal employees during the period of the shutdown is roughly $2.0 billion.*[2] *Total compensation costs, including benefits, are about 30 percent larger, in the range of $2.5 billion.*

Impacts on Programs and Services

An alternative way to quantify the cost of Federal employee furloughs is in terms of their impact on programs and services. Millions of Americans were impacted by the shutdown, due to furloughs of Federal employees, reduced services for the public, and delays in payments to Federal grantees, States, localities, contractors, and individuals. For example, the shutdown:

- Stalled weekly progress in reducing the backlog of veterans' disability claims, which was previously being reduced at a rate of *almost 20,000 claims per week.*
- Delayed *almost $4 billion in tax refunds* and will delay the start of the 2014 tax filing season by *up to two weeks.*
- Prevented *hundreds of patients* from enrolling in National Institutes of Health (NIH) clinical trials.
  o Forced Head Start grantees serving nearly 6,300 children to close their centers for up to nine days (before re-opening with the help of private philanthropists or their state).
  o Delayed home loan decisions for 8,000 rural families.
  o Led the FDA to delay nearly 500 food and feed domestic inspections and roughly 355 food safety inspections under State contracts. These routine inspections enable FDA to determine compliance with law and ensure that unsanitary conditions and practices that may result in foodborne illness are addressed.
  o Prevented the timely and complete investigation of 59 airplane accidents by the National Transportation Safety Board (NTSB).
  o Delayed workshops for 1,400 military service members to help them transition to civilian life and employment.
  o Forced cut-backs in Centers for Disease Control and Prevention (CDC) flu season surveillance and monitoring, leaving local public health authorities without access to complete national flu season data for two weeks.

- o Brought new Federal research activities to a standstill, with 98 percent of National Science Foundation (NSF), nearly three-quarters of NIH, and two-thirds of CDC employees furloughed.
- o Required the National Institutes of Standards and Technology (NIST) and the National Aeronautics and Space Administration (NASA) to furlough four out of the five Nobel Prize-winning researchers currently employed by the Federal government.
- o Halted Environmental Protection Agency (EPA) inspections at about 1200 sites, including hazardous waste facilities, chemical facilities, and drinking water systems.
- o Denied assistance to almost 500 small businesses seeking to keep their workplaces safe, because many States had to shut down the federally-funded Consultation Program.

Costs to the Federal Budget

On top of furloughs, the Federal government also incurred other direct budgetary costs as a result of the shutdown. For example:

- *Fees went uncollected.* For example, the National Park Service estimates that it lost about *$7 million in revenue* as a result of the shutdown, while the Smithsonian lost an additional *$4 million in revenue*.
- *IRS enforcement and other program integrity measures were halted.* The IRS was unable to conduct most enforcement activities during the shutdown, which normally collect *about $1 billion per week*. The Social Security Administration (SSA) was delayed in completing over *1,600 medical disability reviews and over 10,000 Supplemental Security Income (SSI) redeterminations each day*. These reviews ensure that only eligible individuals receive Disability Insurance and SSI benefits.
- *The Federal government will owe interest on late payments.* Under the Prompt Payment Act and the Cash Management Improvement Act, the Federal government will be required to pay interest on billions of dollars of payments that could not be made on time during the shutdown, ranging from IRS refunds to payments to contractors.

- *Agencies incurred personnel and other costs for shutdown implementation.* Even when employees were able to work during the shutdown, thousands of employee hours – and other resources – were diverted to planning for and executing shutdown and startup activities. For example:
    o At the Department of Defense, civilian and military employees at hundreds of installations across the United States and around the world spent thousands of hours developing and implementing plans for managing a shutdown, implementing the Pay Our Military Act, and restarting full operations.
    o The National Nuclear Security Administration (NNSA) at the Department of Energy (DOE) devoted time and resources to placing nuclear weapons labs into safe standby condition, only to direct additional resources to restoring normal operations at these facilities days later.
    o The NSF and its contractors were forced to incur costs to begin placing assets that are part of the U.S. Antarctic Program into caretaker status, in order to safeguard them in the absence of funds to conduct planned research.
    o In a world of diminished program budgets, these shutdown and restart costs came at the expense of support for mission-related work.

Impacts on the Federal Workforce

The recent shutdown jeopardized both the income stability of hundreds of thousands of Federal employees and their ability to focus on important agency missions that citizens rely upon each day.

During the shutdown, hundreds of thousands of Federal employees did not receive their full paychecks, including many employees that were legally required to work during the lapse. While all Federal employees ultimately have been compensated for the period of the shutdown, the burden of delayed paychecks on Federal workers and their families was significant and harmful.

Furloughs during the shutdown also followed an unprecedented three-year pay freeze for Federal employees, and, for hundreds of thousands of workers, administrative furloughs earlier this year caused by sequestration. The shutdown disrupted agency operations in many ways and has been challenging to recover from.

ECONOMIC COST OF THE FEDERAL GOVERNMENT SHUTDOWN

Leading independent forecasters estimate that the shutdown will lower fourth quarter real GDP growth by 0.2-0.6 percentage points or more, or $2-$6 billion in lost output.[3]

- *Standard and Poor's:* "We believe that, to date, the shutdown has shaved at least 0.6% off of annualized fourth-quarter 2013 GDP growth..."[4]
- *Macroeconomic Advisers:* "Calibrating [the 1995-1996 shutdowns] to today's economy, we estimate that a two-week shutdown would directly trim about 0.3 percentage point from fourth quarter growth, mainly by interrupting the flow of services produced by federal employees."[5]
- *Goldman Sachs* projected that the shutdown would reduce GDP growth by 0.14 percentage points per week, even after most furloughed Department of Defense employees returned to work.[6]
- *Mark Zandi, Moody's:* "The 16-day Federal shutdown and political brinksmanship around the Treasury debt ceiling hurt the economy. The hit to fourth quarter real GDP is estimated at... half a percentage point of growth."[7]

However, most of these estimates of the shutdown's economic costs are model-based projections that only take into account how the shutdown affected the direct flow of spending into the economy. There are other factors that should be considered as well, for example:

1. The estimates do not capture any additional costs imposed through the impact of the shutdown on consumer and business confidence.

    - During the shutdown, the Gallup Daily Economic Confidence Index fell to its lowest level since December 2011, likely reflecting the combined impact of the shutdown and debt limit brinksmanship.
    - The October Reuters/Michigan Index of Consumer was at its lowest level since December 2012.

- The Index of Consumer Expectations fell to its lowest level since November 2011.
- A survey commissioned by Goldman Sachs found that two out of five Americans said they would reduce their spending due to the government shutdown.[8]

Using actual high-frequency economic data from the period of the shutdown, the Council of Economic Advisers has estimated that the combination of the Federal government shutdown and debt limit brinksmanship may have reduced fourth-quarter GDP growth by 0.25 percentage points and resulted in 120,000 fewer private sector jobs created between October 1 and October 12.[9] The shutdown lasted until October 16, meaning that the total impact may have been even greater.

2. The projections do not fully capture the direct economic disruption caused by the shutdown of government activities the private sector relies on. For example, the Federal government shutdown:

- Halted permitting and environmental and other reviews, delaying job-creating transportation and energy projects in North Dakota, Wyoming, Utah and other states. The Federal government was unable to issue permits to conduct drilling operations on Federal lands, and it stopped or delayed environmental reviews of planned transportation and energy projects, which prevented companies from moving forward on these projects. In particular, *BLM was unable to process about 200 Applications for Permit to Drill (APDs).* This delayed energy development on Federal lands in North Dakota, Wyoming, Utah and other states. Oil and gas lease sales were also postponed.
- Hindered trade by putting import and export licenses and applications on hold and halting export promotion activities.
  o The Treasury Department's Alcohol and Tobacco Tax and Trade Bureau was unable to issue export certifications for beer, wine, and distilled spirits in response to *100 requests from approximately 65 businesses.* As a result, *more than two million liters of U.S. products were left sitting at ports, unable to ship.*
  o The Department of Commerce's Bureau of Industry and Security *could not accept new export license applications* and *pending*

requests were put on hold, preventing some sellers of high-tech goods from exporting their products.
- o The Export-Import Bank (Ex-Im) suspended approvals of new applications for loans, guarantees, and insurance. In a typical month, Ex-Im approves nearly *$3 billion in authorizations with export value close to $4.2 billion.*
- *Disrupted private-sector lending to individuals and small businesses.* Financial institutions depend on IRS income verification (with taxpayer permission) to determine eligibility for loans such as mortgages. The IRS usually receives close to 400,000 requests per week; *two weeks into the shutdown, IRS had an inventory of 1.2 million requests that could not be processed.* Meanwhile, SSA suspended its consent-based Social Security Number verification system, a system that many financial institutions use to verify Social Security numbers prior to granting credit. This led a number of financial institutions to suspend mortgage processing due to the inability to verify Social Security numbers, according to the Mortgage Bankers Association.
- *Halted Federal loans to small businesses, homeowners, and housing and healthcare facility developers.*
  - o Roughly 700 small businesses applied for roughly $140 million in loans during the shutdown; none of these loans could be approved until the shutdown ended.
  - o FHA delayed processing over 500 applications for loans to develop, rehabilitate, or refinance around 80,000 units of multifamily rental housing.
  - o FHA also suspended the Home Equity Conversion Mortgage (HECM) program, a program that serves seniors who need to draw on their home equity to cover living expenses and medical costs. During a typical two-week period, FHA insures over 2,300 HECM loans.
- *Delayed the Alaskan crab fishing season by three to four days, costing fisherman thousands of dollars in lost revenue.* To prevent unsustainable overfishing, NOAA Fisheries allocate harvest levels and issue permits to fishermen before they can fish. Because the NOAA Fisheries staff were furloughed, fishermen were not able to fish until the government was reopened and these permits were processed, which was 3-4 days after the regularly scheduled start of

the season. Industry estimates that *each lost day led to thousands of dollars of lost revenue* for both the fishing industry and coastal communities, revenue needed to recoup the millions of dollars invested to prepare for the season.

- *Disrupted tourism and travel by closing national parks and the Smithsonian* Normally, National Parks welcome an average of 715,000 visitors a day during October, and these visitors spend an average of $33 million a day, benefiting local communities surrounding the parks. NPS estimates that *the shutdown led to over $500 million in lost visitor spending nationwide,* even after taking into account the 13 parks that were re-opened using state funds after more than a week of being shut down. The park closures also impacted the broader travel industry and local businesses, as families across the country cancelled their travel plans. The travel industry and tourism were also impacted by the Smithsonian closures. For example, the National Gallery of Art receives approximately 12,000 visitors a day on average in the fall, suggesting that *some 200,000 people missed visiting the Gallery during the shutdown.*

- *Significantly impacted small businesses that contract with the Federal government.* Over the first two weeks of the shutdown, *small businesses contracts with DOD were cut by almost one-third and spending was down 40 percent,* compared to the same period in the previous year. Payment delays during the shutdown forced contractors to temporarily lay off employees and imposed particular financial hardship on small businesses with less ability to absorb losses and put off payments of their own.

- *Delayed aircraft purchases and deliveries by closing the FAA's Aircraft Registry.* During the shutdown, aircraft registrations were put on hold due to furloughs of employees at the Office of Aircraft Registry. The General Aviation Manufacturers Association reports that *the shutdown delayed delivery of 156 aircraft deliveries valued at $1.9 billion.* The FAA is currently working to clear the backlog of delayed registrations.

- *Delayed efforts to combat invasive species that are endangering Great Lakes fisheries.* U.S. Geological Survey (USGS) scientists were unable complete field-testing of a technology to prevent the spread of Asian carp into the Great Lakes. The window of opportunity to field test this technology was missed, due to cooling water temperatures, and *testing will now be delayed for six months.* Work was also delayed on other invasive species projects, including research on the spread of dangerous Africanized honeybees in the Southwest, invasive grass species involved in intensifying wildfires, and white-nose bat syndrome impacting bats in national parks.

- *Delayed FDA approval of medical products, devices, and drugs.* In general, no new Fiscal Year (FY) 2014 drug applications, biologics applications, generic drug applications, animal drug applications, or medical device applications sent to the FDA during the shutdown could be accepted, processed, or reviewed. This delayed businesses in moving these products to market.
- *Deprived businesses of important information about the state of the economy.* During the shutdown, Federal statistical agencies were unable to release most economic data and reports. For example:
  o The Bureau of Labor Statistics did not release monthly reports on the Employment Situation, the Producer Price Index, the Consumer Price Index, Real Earnings, or the U.S. Import and Export Price Indexes;
  o The Department of Commerce's Census Bureau and Bureau of Economic Analysis did not release key monthly reports on International Trade, Retail Sales, or Construction;
  o The Energy Information Administration delayed reports including the Principal Economic Indicator for natural gas storage, a report that sets diesel compensation rates for many commercial truckers, a report of heating oil and propane prices faced by many households, and a report assessing petroleum inventories;
  o The National Agricultural Statistics Service postponed, cancelled, or reduced in scope 21 commodity, service, and farm wage reports and data releases; and
  o The release of Census of Agriculture statistical products was postponed.

FEDERAL EMPLOYEE FURLOUGHS

The largest direct cost of the Federal government shutdown – both to the Federal budget and to the economy – was work not performed by Federal employees during the 16-day period. Federal employees were furloughed for a combined total of *6.6 million work days*, with furloughs affecting workers at the vast majority of agencies. Although the October 2013 shutdown was shorter than the 21-day shutdown that took place in December 1995 – January 1996, the total number of employee furlough days was larger, even if one adjusts for growth in the size of the Federal workforce. This is largely because seven appropriations bills were enacted before the start of the December 1995 – January 1996 shutdown, so several major agencies were able to operate normally during that period of time. By contrast, as of October 1, 2013, no agencies had received full Fiscal Year 2014 annual appropriations.

One way to quantify the cost of furloughs is in terms of the amount the Federal government had to pay for work not performed. *We estimate that the total cost of pay due to federal employees furloughed during the shutdown is roughly $2.0 billion; total compensation costs are about 30 percent larger (about $2.5 billion).* This exceeds the comparable payroll costs of $430 million (about $650 million in todays' dollars) for the November 1995 shutdown and $630 million (about $1 billion in today's dollars) for the December 1995 – January 1996 shutdown.[10]

Appendix Table 1 shows the breakdown of furlough days by agency. Overall, Federal agencies furloughed roughly 850,000 employees per day in the immediate aftermath of the lapse in appropriations, or roughly 40 percent of the entire civilian Federal workforce. Those employees that were not furloughed were retained either because they were performing activities that are "excepted" under the applicable legal requirements (such as activities necessary to maintain the safety of life or the protection of property), or because funding remained available to pay their salaries and expenses during the lapse from sources other than annual appropriations.

Because circumstances evolved over the course of the shutdown, there were instances in which agencies modified the number of employees on furlough, both recalling employees and furloughing additional employees. Most notably, after Congress passed and the President signed the Pay Our Military Act, the Department of Defense recalled the majority of the roughly 400,000 civilian employees that were furloughed for the first week of the lapse. (The Pay Our Military Act provided appropriations for the pay and allowances of those civilian personnel that that the Secretary of Defense determined provide support to members of the Armed Forces.)

Changes at other agencies over the course of the shutdown were smaller in magnitude and went in both directions. For example, during the second week of the shutdown, the Social Security Administration recalled over 8,000 workers to process claims appeals and conduct other critical work necessary to ensure the timely payment of benefits. In addition, some employees who were initially working were subsequently furloughed. For instance, over 7,800 employees at the Veterans' Benefits Administration that were working for the first week of the shutdown were furloughed following the exhaustion of remaining carryover balances from the previous fiscal year. The Federal Emergency Management Agency (FEMA) recalled a select number of employees to prepare for Tropical Storm Karen, but the agency subsequently placed these employees back on furlough after the storm dissipated. These changes to the number of furloughed employees reflect the dynamic nature of the shutdown, as agencies responded to changing circumstances over the two and a half weeks.

IMPACTS ON PROGRAMS AND SERVICES

Another way to quantify the costs of Federal employee furloughs is by examining the shutdown's impact on programs and services. The shutdown impacted millions of Americans, due to furloughs of Federal employees, reduced services for the public, and delays in payments to Federal grantees, States, localities, contractors, and individuals. Employees not on the job could not conduct many food, product, and workplace safety inspections, prepare for flu season or monitor other public health issues, or provide numerous other services important to the general public and the economy. Meanwhile, many grantees and contractors not receiving Federal payments during the shutdown furloughed their own employees and delayed or terminated services. The shutdown also affected direct services for veterans, seniors, and other vulnerable groups; public health and basic research; product safety and environmental protection; worker rights and safety; international trade and relations; and other basic government services.

Direct Services for Veterans, Seniors, and Other Vulnerable Groups

- Stalled weekly progress in reducing the veterans' disability claims backlog, which had previously been progressing at a rate of almost 20,000 claims per week. In the six months before the shutdown, the

Department of Veterans Affairs (VA) reduced the disability claims backlog by about 30 percent, and, in the week before the shutdown, VA processed enough applications to reduce the backlog by about 18,000 claims. In contrast, during the two- and a half weeks of the shutdown, the backlog remained roughly flat (at about 418,000 claims).

- Halted or curtailed important veterans' services. Services that help veterans understand their benefits – including the education call center, hotlines, and all regional offices outreach activities – were closed to the public during the shutdown, and many veterans lost access to vocational rehabilitation and education counseling services.
- Delayed access for 1,400 military service members to workshops designed to help them transition to civilian life and employment. The shutdown forced the postponement of some Transition Assistance Program (TAP) workshops, which help transitioning military service members find civilian jobs and access benefits. *40 TAP employment workshops were cancelled and had to be rescheduled, which delayed transition support to 1,400 service members.*
- Temporarily closed six Head Start grantees, serving nearly 6,300 children. *Head start grantees operating in Alabama, Connecticut, Florida, Georgia, Mis sissippi, and South Carolina closed for up to nine days* before reopening with funds provided by philanthropists through the National Head Start Association or their state.
- Delayed home loan decisions for 8,000 low-income working families in rural communities. The Department of Agriculture's single-family loan guarantee program was unable to process loan applications during the shutdown, preventing eligible families from receiving loans.
- Kept home more than 600 young people who had committed a year of their lives to serve local communities through AmeriCorps. AmeriCorps National Civilian Community Corps is a residential program that engages 18- to 24-yearolds in national service, including responding to natural and other disasters such as floods, fires, and tornadoes. More than 600 Corps members who were prepared to begin their service the week of October 6 were told to stay home.

Public Health and Research

- *Cut back flu season surveillance and monitoring, as well as other public health monitoring.* CDC cut back its annual flu vaccination campaign for a period of time and suspended its weekly "Flu View" report, leaving local public health authorities without access to complete national flu season data for two weeks. CDC staff also discontinued analysis of surveillance and molecular epidemiologic data to identify clusters of linked Hepatitis and Tuberculosis cases that cross State or local jurisdictional boundaries.
- *Put on hold most Federal government support for new basic research, due to furloughs of 98 percent of NSF employees, nearly three quarters of the NIH, and two thirds of the CDC.* For example, no new NSF grants or grant continuations were issued during the shutdown; on average, NSF issues about 765 grants and continuations in a two-week period.
- *Furloughed four out of five Nobel Prize-winning researchers currently employed by the Federal government.* Three of the Laureates who were furloughed work at NIST, performing cutting edge research in physics that could have broad commercial applicability in areas such as advanced communications, cyber security, and computing. The fourth furloughed Laureate works at NASA on the new, much more capable, successor to the Hubble Space Telescope. Across agencies, many of the Federal researchers who may contribute to the *next* Nobel Prizewinning discovery in science or medicine were furloughed, with their work delayed or disrupted.
- *Prevented the enrollment of patients in NIH Clinical Center studies.* Although the hospital remained open for patients already enrolled in studies, NIH could not enroll new patients into current studies or start new studies during the shutdown, except for patients with life-threatening or urgent medical problems. During the shutdown, NIH admitted 25 patients, who had a life threatening or urgent medical problem, but seven clinical protocols that were scheduled to begin during the period of the shutdown were delayed.
- *Forced the transition of the NSF's U.S. Antarctic Program (USAP) into caretaker status, resulting in the cancellation of some research activities for the entire 2013-2014 season.* The NSF is responsible for maintaining the United States' presence in the Antarctic, including an

active research program and logistical support for that research. With available funds exhausted after two weeks of the shutdown, NSF began placing USAP research stations, ships and other assets into caretaker status, including redeploying scientific and contracted operations personnel. Caretaker status for the research stations entails minimum human occupancy to ensure protection of government property and safeguarding of human lives. The stations could not be completely shut down because extreme environmental conditions would quickly destroy them. When the government reopened, NSF worked to restore normal operations, but some research and operational activities will have to be cancelled altogether this year. For example, NASA and NSF had to cancel their Antarctic-launched long-duration space science research missions for the year because NSF cannot reopen facilities in time to get research balloons off on schedule. The balloons are used as a platform for space science research into phenomenon such as cosmic rays and the Big Bang.

- *Prevented access to state of the art instruments at NIST that researchers from the private sector and academia rely on.* For example, access was denied to the NIST Center for Neutron Research (NCNR), impacting researchers from academia and industry who had scheduled experiments months in advance. Approximately *70 experiments scheduled at the NCNR months in advance could not be performed. The financial loss due to lost beamtime was approximately $2 million.*

- *Stopped the National Radio Astronomy Observatory's operations at its facilities in Charlottesville, VA, Greenbank, WV, and Socorro, New Mexico, as well as 10 Very Long Baseline Array sites across the United States.* During the shutdown, no new observations were made at these facilities, jeopardizing ongoing projects, especially research requiring continuous data. *Approximately 500 hours of observing time was lost at Green Bank Observatory*; almost half of which was high frequency observing time that is seasonal and cannot be rescheduled. Over 600 hours of observing time were lost at the Very Large Array and Very Long Baseline Array. In addition, observatories *ceased support for approximately 2,700 users who were processing existing data or planning new observations.* This affected a range of projects that detect radio waves emitted by astronomical objects and also advance state-of-the-art signal processing. The loss of time and user support will affect not only researchers, but also undergraduate projects, graduate students seeking data for their thesis projects, and public and school groups whose visits were cancelled.

Product Safety and Environmental Protection

- *Sharply curtailed routine FDA inspections of domestic and international food facilities, delaying nearly 500 food and feed domestic inspections and roughly 355 food safety inspections performed by States under contract.* While the agency continued to conduct "for cause" inspections where there was an imminent threat to health or life, nearly 500 food and feed domestic inspections and roughly 355 state inspections that are normally performed during this period each year did not occur during the shutdown. These routine inspections enable FDA to determine compliance with the law and ensure that unsanitary conditions and practices which may result in foodborne illness are addressed. The FDA also cut back on examination, sampling, and laboratory analysis of imported products during the shutdown.
- *Discontinued FDA oversight of certain non-food products and left consumer questions unanswered.* During the shutdown, the FDA discontinued almost all activities related to the regulation of cosmetics, review of information from manufacturers of medical products (including allergenic extracts, whole blood, and blood components for transfusion), and many user-fee supported human and animal drug, device, or biological product applications. The FDA was also unable to answer routine consumer questions regarding food safety, medical devices, blood products and vaccines, and veterinary products.
- *Prevented the timely and full investigation of 59 airplane accidents by the NTSB.* With the large majority of its workforce furloughed, the NTSB was only able to launch investigations into two aviation accidents during the shutdown, putting it behind schedule for these and other ongoing investigations. The NTSB was also forced to reschedule two important public investigative hearings.
- *Halted the EPA's non-emergency inspections at about 1200 hazardous waste facilities, chemical facilities, and drinking water systems; discontinued evaluations of potential health impacts of new*

- *industrial chemicals; and stopped reviews of pesticides for adverse impacts to health and the environment.* While the majority of these inspections will be rescheduled, they are unlikely to fully be made up during this fiscal year.
- *Stopped Consumer Product Safety Commission (CPSC) work related to recalls of products that could cause injuries.* CPSC was only able to continue work related to products that present an imminent threat to consumer safety, and therefore normal work related to recalls was halted. CPSC's port inspectors were furloughed, preventing the agency from screening thousands of products, including children's merchandise that could contain excessive lead and sleepwear that may violate flammability standards.
- *Prevented the USGS from gathering and processing data on natural disasters.* The USGS lost an opportunity to gather information on damage caused by the Colorado floods, including landslides, debris flows, and other activities. The loss of these data significantly reduces the ability of scientists and disaster response professionals to learn from these extreme events. The shutdown also impacted the capacity of the USGS to deliver information to states on potential pollution caused by record flooding in the South Platte River Basin.

Worker Rights and Safety

- *Suspended almost 1,400 Federal inspections to prevent workplace fatalities and injuries, which will not be fully made up.* The Occupational Safety and Health Administration (OSHA) protects the safety and health of the nation's workers, in part by conducting workplace inspections in high-hazard industries.
During the lapse in appropriations, OSHA could only respond to workplace fatalities, catastrophes and imminent danger situations when there was a high risk of death or serious physical harm. *OSHA opened only 283 total inspections during the shutdown – just 16 percent of the number it opened during same time period last year – and put approximately 1,370 inspections on hold.*
- *Denied assistance to almost 500 small businesses across the country seeking to keep their workplaces safe.* The government shutdown impacted OSHA's Consultation Program, through which States provide free on-site safety and health assistance to small businesses.

One-third of Consultation Programs stopped doing employer visits during the shutdown, impacting almost 500 small businesses.

- *Stopped nearly all investigations to enforce minimum wage, overtime, child labor bans, and other workplace protections.* The Wage and Hour Division (WHD) at the Department of Labor is responsible for enforcing a variety of laws that establish minimum standards for wages and working conditions. In a typical week, WHD concludes more than 600 investigations and compliance actions. However, during the shutdown, WHD was only able to respond to incidents involving imminent serious injury or death of a child or farmworker; as a result, it opened only one new investigation during the two and a half week shutdown and put more than 6,000 ongoing investigations on hold. Over the course of the shutdown, because Wage and Hour investigators were unable to perform their jobs, back wage payments of approximately $8.8 million for an estimated 12,100 workers went uncollected.

- *Delayed ongoing investigation activities surrounding recent workplace safety or casualty events.* Chemical Safety Board investigators were furloughed, halting their analysis of the West, Texas fertilizer plant explosion from April during the shutdown period.

- *Denied a venue for legal relief to thousands of workers experiencing discrimination.* The Equal Employment Opportunity Commission (EEOC) is the primary agency charged with the enforcement of Federal employment discrimination laws. Americans who believe they have experienced discrimination in the workplace must first file charges with the EEOC and await a response before they can file suit in Federal court, and so timely disposition of these charges is critical to EEOC's mission. During the shutdown, EEOC received nearly 3,150 charges of employment discrimination that it was unable to investigate, creating a backlog that it will take about one month to work through.

International Trade and Relations

- *Furloughed nearly all of the Treasury Department's Office of Foreign Asset Control (OFAC), which implements the U.S. government's financial sanctions against countries such as Iran and Syria.* With only a very small share of employees excepted, the office was unable to fully sustain many of its core functions of: (1) issuing new sanctions designations against those enabling the governments of Iran and Syria as well as terrorist organizations, Weapons of Mass Destruction proliferators, narcotics cartels, and transnational organized crime groups; (2) investigating and penalizing sanctions violations; (3) issuing licenses to authorize humanitarian and other important activities that might otherwise be barred by sanctions; and (4) issuing new sanctions prohibitions and guidance. The majority of staff at Treasury Department's Office of Terrorist Financing and Fi nancial Crimes, Office of Intelligence and Analysis, and Financial Crimes Enforcement Network were also furloughed.

- *Cancelled travel by the President and other Administration officials that would have advanced U.S. trade goals and promoted job creation.* The President was forced to cancel a trip to the Asia-Pacific Economic Cooperation (APEC), a trip that could have been a key step in negotiating the Trans-Pacific Partnership regional trade agreement that will link the United States to economies throughout the Asia-Pacific region. U.S. Trade Representative Michael Froman had to postpone a round of negotiations in Brussels on the Transatlantic Trade and Investment Partnership, a trade and investment agreement being negotiated between the European Union and the United States. These trade agreements are critical to opening up markets for U.S. businesses to export goods and services abroad and create jobs at home.

Other Basic Government Services

- *Delayed tax filing assistance and almost $4 billion in refunds to taxpayers.* While continuing to file returns and making estimated payments during the shutdown, taxpayers could not receive assistance from IRS walk-in sites or telephone services, and taxpayer correspondence went unaddressed. Meanwhile, roughly $3.7 billion in refunds (including $2.2 billion in refunds to individuals and $1.5 billion in refunds to businesses) were delayed.

- *Delayed the start of the 2014 tax filing season up to two weeks.* With most IRS operations halted during the shutdown, the IRS could not engage in normal computer programming and testing in preparation for the 2014 tax filing season. As a result, some taxpayers who file early and are entitled to refunds may have their refunds delayed for up to two weeks due to the delay of the start of the originally planned 2014 tax filing season.
- *Suspended the issuance of Social Security cards and closed down the E-Verify system for employers to check worker eligibility.* On a typical day, approximately 60,000 Americans apply for Social Security cards, which they may need to be able to start a job, take out a loan, open a bank account, or conduct other financial transactions. During the shutdown, SSA could not issue new Social Security cards. Employers were also unable to access the E-Verify system to check prospective employees' immigration status.

OTHER DIRECT BUDGETARY COSTS

On top of furloughs, shutdown implementation costs, and reductions to key programs and services, the Federal government also incurred other direct budgetary costs as a result of the shutdown. These included:

- *Uncollected fees.* The National Park Service estimates that it was unable to collect about *$450,000 per day* in revenue from entrance fees, campgrounds, tours, and special uses, for a total cost of roughly *$7 million in lost revenue.* In addition, the closure of the Smithsonian resulted in an additional *$4 million in lost revenue.* This is from lost museum-based revenue from stores and theaters, lost revenue from the National Zoo shops/concessions, and lost special events revenue.
- *Program Integrity Activities.* Program integrity activities generally had to be suspended during the shutdown, despite the fact that these measures save money over the long run. The shutdown halted most IRS enforcement activities, which collect $1 billion per week on average. In addition, SSA was delayed in completing over 1,600 medical disability reviews and over 10,000 Supplemental Security Income (SSI) redeterminations each day. Medical disability reviews assess whether individuals are still medically eligible for disability

benefits, while SSI redeterminations review whether beneficiaries meet SSI's non-medical eligibility factors, such as income and asset limits, and ensure that beneficiaries are paid the correct amounts.

- *Interest due on late payments.* Under the Prompt Payment Act and the Cash Management Improvement Act, the federal government is required to pay interest on payments due to third parties when it fails to pay these bills on time. The government will owe interest on billions of dollars of payments not made on time during the shutdown, ranging from IRS refunds to contractor payments.
- *Contract Workforce.* The shutdown resulted in over 10,000 stop work orders for contracts and numerous temporary layoffs among the federal contractor community. Federal acquisition regulations allow contractors to request equitable adjustments for certain cost impacts associated with having to put operations on hold (e.g., costs of maintaining idle facilities, unabsorbed overhead). There could be thousands of requests from contractors seeking to be reimbursed for costs incurred as a result of these suspensions.

In addition, simply implementing the government shutdown and re-start activities imposed significant costs, diverting employee hours and agency resources from mission- critical functions. While a comprehensive estimate of these costs is not available, examples include:

- At the Department of Defense, civilian and military employees at hundreds of installations across the United States and around the world spent *thousands of hours* developing and implementing plans for managing a lapse in appropriations, implementing the Pay Our Military Act, and restarting full operations.
- The Department of Energy and its contractors devoted significant resources to placing labs and project sites into safe standby condition and then returning them to operational status. For example:
  o Restoring normal operations at the National Nuclear Security Administration can take more than a week and labs and plants are likely to have lost at least *three weeks of mission work*, or about *6 percent of the year's productivity*, due to the shutdown.
  o Similarly, disruptions at nuclear cleanup sites associated with the shutdown will cost *two to three weeks of productivity*, and may

cause the Department of Energy to miss cleanup milestones agreed to with the states where cleanup is under way.
- The NSF and its contractors incurred significant costs to begin placing assets that are part of the U.S. Antarctic Program and other major research facilities into caretaker status, to safeguard them in the absence of funds to conduct planned research. NSF is now incurring additional costs to reopen these facilities and restart research to the extent possible.
- The Department of Transportation (DOT) has estimated that it will incur additional *costs of around $325,000* associated with closing and reopening the US Merchant Marine Academy. Because of the shutdown, the US Merchant Marine Academy had to shut down classes for nearly three weeks. This will have a ripple effect throughout the school year, as midshipmen make up lost sea and class time. DOT will incur costs for staff overtime and to transport Midshipmen back to campus.

IMPACTS ON THE FEDERAL WORKFORCE

The shutdown jeopardized both the income stability of Federal employees and their ability to focus on important agency missions that citizens rely upon each day.

During the shutdown, hundreds of thousands of Federal employees did not receive their full paychecks, including many who were legally required to work during the lapse. Also, due to expiration of a statutory provision that was in effect during the shutdown in 1995- 1996, excepted employees (who were legally required to work during the lapse) were not eligible to apply for unemployment benefits to help meet any immediate cash flow needs. While all Federal employees have now been compensated for the period of the shutdown, the burden this placed on families was significant and avoidable.

It is also important to note that the shutdown came on top of an unprecedented three-year pay freeze for Federal employees as well as furloughs and other reductions that resulted from sequestration earlier this year.

The shutdown and sequestration-related furloughs risk undermining the competitive advantage government agencies have traditionally used in recruiting and retaining a talented workforce – income stability provided by civil service jobs, and a calling to the important work of public service. Notably, surveys have shown that compensation and the nature of the work are the top two considerations of students as they weigh job options.[11] This allows the government to be competitive for many high skill jobs where the private sector enjoys other advantages.

Reports from news outlets highlighted the challenges shutdown presents for both retaining current employees and the recruiting top talent for the future. For example, as one EPA employee told the Washington Post "We love public service. We're very committed to our jobs and the mission of our agency. But it's just too unstable."[12] Federal contractors are also worried about hiring in an environment of heightened uncertainty. Gregory Bloom, the president of a small business that works on design and engineering for NASA, told the Washington Post, "Trying to get the best and the brightest to come join a company that specializes in national defense or NASA-supported activities and not being able to tell them that they're going to have a job in six months is a real tricky challenge for us. What keeps coming back to us is 'why go work in national defense or aerospace when we can go to Google and know that we're going to have a job?'"[13]

Studies have shown that – above all else – employees of all stripes value an ability to make progress each day in their job. The Federal government is fortunate to have such a high percent of its employees willing to put in extra effort to get a job done (96 percent in the latest survey). However, at the end of the day, the government shutdown risks seriously damaging the ability to attract and retain the kind of driven, patriotic Americans to public service that our citizens deserve and that our system of self-government demands.

Table 1. Estimated Employee Furlough Days by Agency

Major Agencies	Total Employee Furlough Days (Thousands)
Department of Defense	1,600
Department of the Treasury	985
Department of Agriculture	737
Department of the Interior	646
Department of Health and Human Services	449
Department of Commerce	312
Department of Homeland Security	303

Major Agencies	Total Employee Furlough Days (Thousands)
Department of Justice	200
Department of Transportation	198
National Aeronautics and Space Administration	192
Environmental Protection Agency	167
Social Security Administration	150
Department of Labor	147
Department of Housing and Urban Development	91
General Services Administration	85
Department of Veterans' Affairs	77
Smithsonian	62
Department of Education	44
Small Business Administration	24
Equal Employment Opportunity Commission	23
National Archives and Records Administration	21
Federal Communications Commission	19
National Labor Relations Board	18
Nuclear Regulatory Commission	18
National Science Foundation	16
Executive Office of the President	14
Broadcasting Board of Governors	7
Commodity Futures Trading Corporation	7
Office of Personnel Management	7
Corporation for National and Community Service	6
Railroad Retirement Board	5
Export-Import Bank	4
Department of State	4
Federal Deposit Insurance Corporation	1
Department of Energy	1
Government-Wide Total	roughly 6.6 million

End Notes

[1] Council of Economic Advisers, "Economic Activity During the Government Shutdown and Debt Limit Brinksmanship," October 2013, http://www.whitehouse.gov/sites/default/files/docs/weekly indicators report final.pdf.

[2] This estimate is based on average salary costs for furloughed employees by agency. It includes only costs for normal work days (excluding weekends and Columbus Day).

[3] Some have reported this output loss on an annualized basis, in which case it amounts to up to $24 billion.

[4] Standard and Poor's, October 16, 2013.

[5] Macroeconomic Advisers, on behalf of the Peterson Foundation, "The Costs of Crisis-Driven Fiscal Policy," October 2013.

[6] Goldman Sachs Global Economics, "Shutdown Continues But Recent Actions Are Likely to Reduce Economic Effects," October 6, 2013.

[7] Mark Zandi, "A Budget Battle Postmortem," Moody's Analytics, October 2013.

[8] Minsi Chung, "Two Out of Five Americans Cut Spending Amid Government Shutdown," Bloomberg, October 15, 2013.

[9] Council of Economic Advisers, "Economic Activity During the Government Shutdown and Debt Limit Brinksmanship," October 2013, http://www.whitehouse.gov/sites/default/files/docs/weeklyindicators report final.pdf.

[10] Following the two shutdowns in Fiscal Year 1996, OMB calculated a combined cost to the Federal government of $1.4 billion ($430 million in payroll costs from the November shutdown, $630 million in payroll costs from the December-January shutdown, and $300 million in other Federal costs.)

[11] National Association of Colleges and Employers' 2012 Student Survey Report, accessed October 18, 2013

[12] Hendrix, Steve. Halved Paychecks Force the Furloughed to Slash Expenses and Take Loans, Second Jobs; The Washington Post. October 10, 2013. Accessed on October 18, 2013 at http://articles.washingtonpost.com/2013-10-10/local/42902098_1_second-jobs-retirement-savings-paychecks

[13] Yeager, Holly. Federal Shutdown Starts Affecting America Beyond Government Workers; The Standard Examiner. October 11, 2013. Accessed on October 18, 2013 at http://www.standard.net/stories/2013/10/11/federal-shutdown-starts-affecting-america-beyond-government-workers

In: The Government Shutdown of 2013
Editor: Rosanne C. Lundy

ISBN: 978-1-63117-112-3
© 2014 Nova Science Publishers, Inc.

Chapter 4

FEDERAL FUNDING GAPS: A BRIEF OVERVIEW[*]

Jessica Tollestrup

SUMMARY

The Antideficiency Act (31 U.S.C. 1341-1342, 1511-1519) generally bars the obligation of funds in the absence of appropriations. Exceptions are made under the act, including for activities involving "the safety of human life or the protection of property." The interval during the fiscal year when appropriations for a particular project or activity are not enacted into law, either in the form of a regular appropriations act or a continuing resolution (CR), is referred to as a *funding gap*. Although funding gaps may occur at the start of the fiscal year, they also may occur any time a CR expires and another CR (or the regular appropriations bill) is not enacted immediately thereafter. Multiple funding gaps may occur within a fiscal year.

When a funding gap occurs, federal agencies are generally required to begin a *shutdown* of the affected projects and activities, which includes the prompt furlough of non-excepted personnel. The general practice of the federal government after the shutdown has ended has been to retroactively pay furloughed employees for the time they missed, as well as employees who were required to come to work.

---

[*] This is an edited, reformatted and augmented version of a Congressional Research Service publication, CRS Report for Congress RS20348, prepared for Members and Committees of Congress, from www.crs.gov, dated October 29, 2013.

Although a shutdown may be the result of a funding gap, the two events should be distinguished. This is because a funding gap may result in a total shutdown of all affected projects or activities in some instances, but not others. For example, when funding gaps are of a short duration, agencies may not have enough time to complete a shutdown of affected projects and activities before funding is restored. In addition, the Office of Management and Budget has previously indicated that a shutdown of agency operations within the first day of the funding gap may be postponed if a resolution appears to be imminent.

Since FY1977, 18 funding gaps occurred, ranging in duration from one day to 21 full days. These funding gaps are listed in *Table 1*. About half of these funding gaps were brief (i.e., three days or less in duration). Notably, many of the funding gaps that occurred during this period do not appear to have resulted in a "shutdown." Prior to the issuance of the opinions in 1980 and early 1981 by then-Attorney General Benjamin Civiletti, while agencies tended to curtail some operations in response to a funding gap, they often "continued to operate during periods of expired funding." In addition, some of the funding gaps after the Civiletti opinions did not result in a completion of shutdown operations, due to both the funding gap's short duration and an expectation that appropriations would soon be enacted. Some of the funding gaps during this period, however, did have a broader impact on affected government operations, even if only for a matter of hours.

Two of the three most recent funding gaps occurred in FY1996, which amounted to five days and 21 days. The chronology of regular and continuing appropriations enacted during FY1996 is illustrated in *Figure 1*.

The most recent funding gap commenced at the beginning of FY2014, on October 1, 2013, and concluded on October 17, 2013, for a total of 16 days.

BACKGROUND

The routine activities of most federal agencies are funded annually by one or more of the regular appropriations acts. When action on the regular appropriations acts is delayed, a continuing appropriations act, also sometimes referred to as a *continuing resolution* or CR, may be used to provide interim budget authority. Measures providing continuing appropriations usually take the form of a joint resolution, rather than a bill.[1]

Since FY1952, all of the regular appropriations acts were enacted by the beginning of the fiscal year in only four instances (FY1977, FY1989, FY1995, and FY1997). No CRs were enacted for three of these fiscal years, but CRs were enacted for FY1977 to fund certain unauthorized programs whose funding had been dropped from the regular appropriations acts.[2] Further, no CRs were enacted for FY1953, even though all but one of the regular appropriations was enacted after the start of the fiscal year.[3]

The Antideficiency Act (31 U.S.C. 1341-1342, 1511-1519) generally bars the obligation or expenditure of federal funds in the absence of appropriations.[4] Exceptions are made under the act, including for activities involving "the safety of human life or the protection of property."[5] The interval during the fiscal year when appropriations for a particular project or activity are not enacted into law, either in the form of a regular appropriations act or a CR, is referred to as a *funding gap*.[6] Although funding gaps may occur at the start of the fiscal year, they also may occur any time a CR expires, and another CR (or the relevant regular appropriations bill) is not enacted immediately thereafter. Multiple funding gaps may occur within a fiscal year.

In 1980 and early 1981, then-Attorney General Benjamin Civiletti issued opinions (hereafter, "the Civiletti opinions") clarifying the need for the federal government to begin terminating regular activities upon the occurrence of a funding gap.[7] As a consequence of these more strict guidelines, when a funding gap occurs, executive agencies begin a *shutdown* of the affected projects and activities, which includes the prompt furlough of non-excepted personnel.[8] The general practice of the federal government after the shutdown has ended has been to retroactively pay furloughed employees for the time they missed, as well as employees who were required to come to work.[9]

Under current practice, although a shutdown may be the result of a funding gap, the two events should be distinguished. This is because a funding gap may result in a shutdown of all affected projects or activities in some instances, but not in others. For example, when a funding gap is of a short duration, agencies may not have enough time to complete a shutdown of affected projects and activities before funding is restored. In addition, the Office of Management and Budget has previously indicated that a shutdown of agency operations within the first day of a funding gap may be postponed if it appears that an additional CR or regular appropriations is likely to be enacted that same day.[10]

To avoid funding gaps, proposals have previously been offered to establish an "automatic continuing resolution" (ACR) that would provide a fallback source of funding for activities, at a specified formula or level, in the event the timely enactment of appropriations is disrupted.[11] The funding would become available automatically and remain available as long as needed so that a funding gap would not occur. Although the House and Senate have considered ACR proposals in the past, none have been enacted into law on permanent basis.

FUNDING GAPS SINCE FY1977

As illustrated in *Table 1,* there have been 18 funding gaps since FY1977.[12] The enactment of a CR on the day after the budget authority in the previous CR expired, which has occurred often, is not counted in this report as involving a funding gap. For example, between FY2000-FY2013, "next-day" CRs were enacted 18 times.

Almost all of the funding gaps occurred between FY1977 and FY1995. During this 19-fiscal-year period, 15 funding gaps occurred.

Multiple funding gaps occurred during a single fiscal year in four instances: (1) three gaps covering a total of 28 days in FY1978; (2) two gaps covering a total of four days in FY1983; (3) two gaps covering a total of three days in FY1985; and (4) two gaps covering a total of 26 days in FY1996.

Seven of the funding gaps commenced with the beginning of the fiscal year on October 1. The remaining 11 funding gaps occurred at least more than one day after the fiscal year had begun. Ten of the funding gaps ended in October, four ended in November, three ended in December, and one ended in January.[13]

Funding gaps have ranged in duration from one to 21 full days. Six of the eight lengthiest funding gaps, lasting between 8 days and 17 days, occurred between FY1977 and FY1980, before the Civiletti opinions were issued in 1980 and early 1981. After the issuance of these opinions, the duration of funding gaps in general shortened considerably, typically ranging from one day to three days. Of these, most occurred over a weekend.

Notably, many of the funding gaps that occurred since FY1977 do not appear to have resulted in a "shutdown." Prior to the issuance of the Civiletti opinions, while agencies tended to curtail some operations in response to a funding gap, they often "continued to operate during periods of expired funding."[14] In addition, some of the funding gaps after the Civiletti opinions did not result in a completion of shutdown operations, due to both a funding gap's short duration and an expectation that appropriations would soon be enacted. For example, during the three-day FY1984 funding gap, "no disruption to government services" reportedly occurred, due to both the three-day holiday weekend and the expectation that appropriations passed by the

House and Senate during that weekend would soon be signed into law by the President.[15]

Table 1. Appropriations Funding Gaps Since FY1977

Fiscal Year	Final Date of Budget Authority[a]	Full Day(s) of Gaps[b]	Date Gap Terminated[c]
1977	Thursday, 09/30/76	10	Monday, 10/11/76
1978	Friday, 09/30/77	12	Thursday, 10/13/77
	Monday, 10/31/77	8	Wednesday, 11/09/77
	Wednesday, 11/30/77	8	Friday, 12/09/77
1979	Saturday, 09/30/78	17	Wednesday, 10/18/78
1980	Sunday, 09/30/79	11	Friday, 10/12/79
1982	Friday, 11/20/81	2	Monday, 11/23/81
1983	Thursday, 09/30/82	1	Saturday, 10/02/82
	Friday, 12/17/82	3	Tuesday, 12/21/82
1984	Thursday, 11/10/83	3	Monday, 11/14/83
1985	Sunday, 09/30/84	2	Wednesday, 10/03/84
	Wednesday, 10/03/84	1	Friday, 10/05/84
1987	Thursday, 10/16/86	1	Saturday, 10/18/86
1988	Friday, 12/18/87	1	Sunday, 12/20/87
1991	Friday, 10/05/90	3	Tuesday, 10/09/90
1996	Monday, 11/13/95	5	Sunday, 11/19/95
	Friday, 12/15/95	21	Saturday, 01/06/96
2014	Monday, 09/30/13	16	Thursday, 10/17/14

Source: Compiled by CRS with data from the Legislative Information System of the U.S. Congress.

[a] Budget authority expired at the end of the date indicated. For example, for the first FY1996 funding gap, budget authority expired at the end of the day on Monday, November 13, 1995, and the funding gap of five full days commenced on Tuesday, November 14, 1995. The enactment of a CR on the day after the previous CR expired, which has occurred often, is not counted as involving a funding gap.

[b] Full days are counted as beginning after the final day on which budget authority was available, and ending the day before the gap terminated. For example, for the first FY1996 funding gap, the full days of the gap were from November 14, 1995, through November 18, 1995, for a total of five full days.

[c] Gap terminated due to the enactment of a continuing resolution, or one or more regular appropriations acts.

Some of the funding gaps during this period, however, did have a broader impact on affected government operations, even if only for a matter of hours.

For example, in response to the one-day funding gap that occurred on October 4, 1984, a furlough of non-excepted personnel for part of that day was reportedly implemented.[16] The three most recent funding gaps, two in FY1996 and one in FY2014, all resulted in a cessation of non-excepted activities and furlough of associated personnel. The legislative history and agency response to these three funding gaps are summarized below.

FY1996

The two FY1996 funding gaps occurred between November 13-19, 1995, and December 15, 1995, through January 6, 1996. The chronology of regular and continuing appropriations enacted during that fiscal year is illustrated in *Figure 1*. In the lead-up to the first funding gap, only three out of the 13 regular appropriations acts had been signed into law[17] and budget authority, which had been provided by a CR[18] since the start of the fiscal year, expired at the end of the day on November 13. On this same day, President Clinton vetoed a CR[19] that would have extended budget authority through December 1, 1995, because of the Medicare premium increases contained within the measure.[20] The ensuing funding gap reportedly resulted in the furlough of an estimated 800,000 federal workers.[21] After five days, a deal was reached to end the shutdown and extend funding via two CRs through December 15.[22] Agencies that had been zeroed out in pending appropriations bills were funded at a rate of 75% of FY1995 budget authority. All other agencies were funded at the lower of the House- or Senate-passed level of funding contained in the FY1996 full-year appropriations bills. The CR also contained an agreement between President Clinton and Congress regarding future negotiations to lower the budget deficit within seven years.[23]

During the first FY1996 funding gap and prior to the second one, an additional four regular appropriations measures were enacted, and three others were vetoed.[24] The negotiations on the six remaining bills were unsuccessful before the budget authority contained within the CR expired at the end of the day on December 15, 1995.[25] Reportedly, about 280,000 executive branch employees were furloughed during the funding gap between December 15, 1995, and January 6, 1996.[26] A CR to provide benefits for veterans and welfare recipients and to keep the District of Columbia government operating was passed and signed into law on December 22, 1995.[27]

Federal Funding Gaps: A Brief Overview

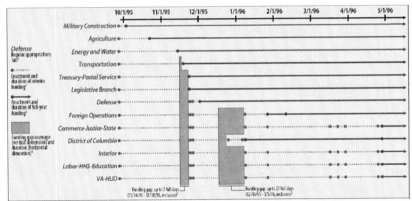

Source: CRS Report R42647, Continuing Resolutions: Overview of Components and Recent Practices, by Jessica Tollestrup, and CRS analysis of public laws available through the Legislative Information System (LIS, lis.gov).

1. In FY1996, the annual appropriations process anticipated the enactment of 13 "regular appropriations" bills.
2. Interim funding was provided through 13 continuing resolutions (CRs) of varying coverage and duration. For a list of these continuing resolutions and their enactment dates, see Table 4 in CRS Report R42647, Continuing Resolutions: Overview of Components and Recent Practices, by Jessica Tollestrup.
3. Full-year funding was provided through eight regular appropriations acts (P.L. 104-32, P.L. 104-37, P.L. 104-46, P.L. 104-50, P.L. 104-52, P.L. 104-53, P.L. 104-61, and P.L. 104-107), two full-year CRs (P.L. 104-92 and P.L. 104-99), and an omnibus appropriations act (P.L. 104-134). For Foreign Operations and District of Columbia, although full-year funding was initially provided in CRs, final action on annual appropriations (P.L. 104-107 and P.L. 104-134) superseded that funding.
4. The "coverage" of the funding gap refers to those regular appropriations bills that had not been enacted during all or some of the days during which the funding gap occurred. The "duration" of the funding gap is calculated here as the number of full days affected by the lapse in funding. Full days are counted as beginning after the final day on which budget authority was available, and ending the day before funding resumed.
5. Interim funding was enacted late in the day on November 19, 1995 (P.L. 104-54). As a consequence, in many instances agency operations may not have restarted until the following day.
6. Three interim funding measures included full-year funding for certain activities (P.L. 104-69, P.L. 104-91, and P.L. 104-92). However, this provision of agency- or program-specific, full-year funding is not reflected in the figure, which focuses on the enactment of entire regular appropriations bills.

Figure 1. Chronology of FY1996 Appropriations.

The shutdown officially ended on January 6, 1996, when the first of a series of CRs to reopen federal government and provide budget authority through January 26, 1996,[28] was enacted.[29]

FY2014

The most recent funding gap commenced at the beginning of FY2014, on October 1, 2013. None of the 12 regular appropriations bills for FY2014 were enacted prior to the beginning of the funding gap. In addition, as of the beginning of the fiscal year, an interim CR to provide budget authority for the projects and activities covered by those 12 bills was also not enacted. On September 30, however, an automatic continuing resolution was enacted to cover FY2014 pay and allowances for (1) certain members of the Armed Forces, (2) certain Department of Defense (DOD) civilian personnel, and (3) other specified DOD and Department of Homeland Security contractors (H.R. 3210; P.L. 113-39, 113th Congress).[30]

At the beginning of this 16-day funding gap, more than 800,000 executive branch employees were reportedly furloughed.[31] This number was reduced during the course of the funding gap due to the implementation of P.L. 113-39 and other redeterminations of whether certain employees were excepted from furlough.[32] Prior to the resolution of the funding gap, congressional action on appropriations was generally limited to a number of narrow CRs to provide funding for certain programs or classes of individuals.[33] Of these, only the Department of Defense Survivor Benefits Continuing Appropriations Resolution of 2014 (H.J.Res. 91; P.L. 113-44) was enacted into law.

On October 16, 2013, the Senate passed H.R. 2775, which had been previously passed by the House on September 12, with an amendment. This amendment, in part, provided interim continuing appropriations for the previous year's programs and activities through January 15, 2014. Later that same day, the House agreed to the Senate amendment to H.R. 2775. The CR was signed into law on October 17, 2013 (P.L. 113-46), thus terminating the funding gap.

End Notes

[1] For a discussion of continuing resolutions generally, see CRS Report R42647, Continuing Resolutions: Overview of Components and Recent Practices, by Jessica Tollestrup.

[2] P.L. 94-473 made continuing appropriations through March 31, 1977. P.L. 95-16 extended the date of the budget authority contained within P.L. 94-473 through April 30, 1977.

[3] Section 1414 of P.L. 82-547 (66 Stat. 661, which was enacted on July 15, 1952, made regular appropriations retroactively available as of July 1 (the first day of FY1953), and ratified any obligations incurred prior to the law's enactment.

[4] The Antideficiency Act is discussed in CRS Report RL30795, General Management Laws: A Compendium, by Clinton T. Brass et al. In addition, the Government Accountability Office provides information about the act online at http://www.gao.gov/ada/antideficiency.htm.

[5] See 31 U.S.C. §1342. During a funding gap, personnel and related activities that are determined to be necessary for the "the safety of human life or the protection of property," or fall under other allowable exceptions, are referred to as "excepted." Under Department of Justice guidance (discussed later in this report), agencies may incur obligations ahead of appropriations for these "excepted" purposes.

[6] In most cases, funding provided in regular appropriations acts is available to be obligated only in a single fiscal year, so that in the event that no subsequent budget authority is provided, agencies may not enter into further obligations. In these instances, budget authority that had previously been enacted and available for obligation for longer periods (e.g., multi-year or "no-year" appropriations) would generally remain available.

[7] The text of the opinions is included in Appendices IV and VIII to the then General Accounting Office (now Government Accountability Office; GAO) report, Funding Gaps Jeopardize Federal Government Operations, PAD-81-31, March 3, 1981.

[8] While, to some extent, what constitutes a "shutdown" may be in the eye of the beholder, it could be argued that, at a minimum, a shutdown would involve agency efforts to distinguish between excepted and non-excepted personnel, to cease non-excepted activities, and furlough associated personnel. For further discussion of what constitutes a "shutdown," see CRS Report RL34680, Shutdown of the Federal Government: Causes, Processes, and Effects, coordinated by Clinton T. Brass.

[9] For a discussion of federal government shutdowns, see CRS Report RL34680, Shutdown of the Federal Government: Causes, Processes, and Effects, coordinated by Clinton T. Brass.

[10] See, for example, Executive Office of the President, Office of Management and Budget, "Planning for Agency Operations During a Lapse in Government Funding," memorandum from Jacob J. Lew, Director of Office of Management and Budget, M-11-13, April 7, 2011, p. 3, and Executive Office of the President, Office of Management and Budget, "Anticipated Enactment of a Continuing Resolution," memorandum from Jacob J. Lew, Director of Office of Management and Budget, M-11-14, April 8, 2011.

[11] For more information on this topic, see CRS Report R41948, Automatic Continuing Resolutions: Background and Overview of Recent Proposals, by Jessica Tollestrup.

[12] FY1977 marked the first full implementation of the congressional budget process established by the Congressional Budget Act of 1974, which moved the beginning of the fiscal year to October 1.

[13] The enactment of a series of continuing resolutions for a fiscal year is discussed in CRS Report R42647, Continuing Resolutions: Overview of Components and Recent Practices, by Jessica Tollestrup.

[14] GAO, Funding Gaps Jeopardize Federal Government Operations, PAD-81-31, March 3, 1981, p. 2. GAO further stated that, "Short of telling employees not to show up for work, Federal officials have responded to gaps by cutting or postponing all non-essential obligations— particular personnel actions, travel, and the award of new contracts—in an attempt to continue the operations of programs for which they are responsible." Media reports related

to funding gaps prior to FY1982 also suggest that little or no shutdown occurred. See, for example, "Continued Funding, 1977," Congressional Quarterly Almanac, vol. XXXII, pp. 789-790; "Conferees Inch Toward Abortion Agreement," CQ Weekly, October 1, 1977, p. 2084; "Payroll Crisis Is Staved Off and HEW, Labor," Washington Post, October 14, 1977; "Congress fails to make appropriations deadline," National Journal, October 8, 1977; "Abortion Agreement Ends Funding Deadlock," Congressional Quarterly Weekly, December 10, 1977, p. 2547; "Funding Lags as Fiscal Year Begins," Washington Post, October 3, 1978; "Congress Fails to Make Appropriations Deadline," National Journal , October 8, 1977, p. 1587; and "Pay, Abortion Issues Delay Hill Funding Bills," Congressional Quarterly Almanac, vol. XXXV, pp. 270-277.

[15] "Congress Clears 2nd Continuing Resolution," Congressional Quarterly Almanac vol. XXXIX, 1983, pp. 528-531.

[16] For further information, see "Last-Minute Money Bill Was Largest Ever," Congressional Quarterly Almanac, vol. XXXX pp. 444-447; Robert Pear, "Senate Works Past Deadline on Catchall Government Spending Bill," New York Times, October 4, 1984, p. A29; and Monica Borkowski, "Looking Back; Previous Government Shutdowns," New York Times, November 11, 1995.

[17] The Military Construction Appropriations Act, H.R. 1817 (P.L. 104-32), was enacted on October 3, 1995. The Agriculture, Rural Development, Food and Drug Administration, and Related Agencies Appropriations Act, H.R. 1976 (P.L. 104-37), was enacted on October 21, 1995. The Energy and Water Development Appropriations Act, H.R. 1905 (P.L. 104-46), was enacted on November 13, 1995. The Legislative Branch Appropriations Act, H.R. 1854 (104th Cong.) was vetoed on October 12, 1995. As of the end of the day on November 13, 1995, the ten regular appropriations bills that had yet to be enacted were the (1) Department of Transportation and Related Agencies Appropriations Act, (2) Treasury, Postal Service, and General Government Appropriations Act, (3) Legislative Branch Appropriations Act, (4) Department of Defense Appropriations Act, (5) Department of Interior and Related Agencies Appropriations Act, (6) Department of Veterans Affairs and Housing and Urban Development, and Independent Agencies Appropriations Act, (7) Department of Commerce and Related Agencies Appropriations Act, (8) Foreign Operations, Export Financing, and Related Programs Appropriations Act, (9) Departments of Labor, Health and Human Services, and Education, and Related Agencies Appropriations Act, and (10) District of Columbia Appropriations Act.

[18] H.J.Res. 108 (P.L. 104-31).

[19] H.J.Res. 115 (1044th Cong.).

[20] Message to the House of Representatives Returning Without Approval Continuing Resolution Legislation," November 13, 1995, William J. Clinton, Public Papers of the Presidents of the United States, 1995, Book 2, July 1 to December 31, 1995, p. 1755. See also "Clinton Vetoes Stopgap Bill to Keep Federal Government Open," CQ Today, November 14, 1995.

[21] For example, see U.S. Congress, House Committee on Government Reform and Oversight, Subcommittee on Civil Service, Government Shutdown I: What's Essential? hearings, 104th Cong., 1st sess., December 6 and 14, 1995 (Washington: GPO, 1997), pp. 6 and 265.

[22] H.J.Res. 123 (P.L. 104-54), H.J.Res. 122 (P.L. 104-56).

[23] For a summary of the first FY1996 funding gap and government shutdown, see "Overview: Government Shuts Down Twice Due to Lack of Funding," Congressional Quarterly Almanac, 104th Cong., 1st sess. (1995), vol. LI, pp. 11-3 through 11-6; "Special Report – Budget Showdown: Day by Day," CQ Weekly, November 18, 1995.

[24] The Department of Transportation and Related Agencies Appropriations Act, H.R. 2002 (P.L. 104-50), was enacted on November 15, 1995. The Treasury, Postal Service, and General Government Appropriations Act, H.R. 2020 (P.L. 104-52), was enacted on November 19, 1995. The Legislative Branch Appropriations Act, H.R. 2492 (P.L. 104-53) was enacted on November 19, 1995. The Department of Defense Appropriations Act, H.R. 2126 (P.L. 104-61), was enacted on December 1, 1995. The Department of Interior and Related Agencies Appropriations Act, H.R. 1977 (104th Cong.), was vetoed on December 18, 1995. The Department of Veterans Affairs and Housing and Urban Development, and Independent Agencies Appropriations Act, H.R. 2099 (104th Cong.), was vetoed on December 18, 1995. The Department of Commerce and Related Agencies Appropriations Act, H.R. 2076 (104th Cong.), was vetoed on December 19, 1995.

[25] As of the end of the day on December 15, 1995, the six regular appropriations bills that had yet to be enacted were the (1) Department of Interior and Related Agencies Appropriations Act, (2) Department of Veterans Affairs and Housing and Urban Development, and Independent Agencies Appropriations Act, (3) Department of Commerce and Related Agencies Appropriations Act, (4) Foreign Operations, Export Financing, and Related Programs Appropriations Act, (5) Departments of Labor, Health and Human Services, and Education, and Related Agencies Appropriations Act, and (6) District of Columbia Appropriations Act.

[26] For further information on the effects of the second FY1996 funding gap, see Dan Moran and Stephen Barr, "When Shutdown Hit Home Ports, GOP Cutters Trimmed Their Sails," Washington Post, January 8, 1996.

[27] H.J.Res. 136 (P.L. 104-69).

[28] H.J.Res. 134 (P.L. 104-94). H.R. 1358 (P.L. 104-91) and H.R. 1643 (P.L. 104-92) were also enacted on January 6. These two CRs provided budget authority for some federal government activities until the end of FY1996.

[29] For a summary of the second FY1996 funding gap and government shutdown, see "Overview: Government Shuts down Twice Due to Lack of Funding," Congressional Quarterly Almanac, 104th Cong., 1st sess. (1995), vol. LI, pp. 11- 3 through 11-6; "Funding Expires Again in Budget Stalemate." CQ Weekly, December 23, 1995; "Congress Clears Bills to Reopen Government," CQ Today, January 8, 1996.

[30] For further information with regard to the operation of P.L. 113-39 (H.R. 3210, 113th Cong.) during the FY2014 funding gap, see CRS Report R41745, Government Shutdown: Operations of the Department of Defense During a Lapse in Appropriations, by Amy Belasco and Pat Towell and CRS Report R43252, FY2014 Appropriations Lapse and the Department of Homeland Security: Impact and Legislation, by William L. Painter. For further information with regard to ACRs generally, see CRS Report R41948, Automatic Continuing Resolutions: Background and Overview of Recent Proposals, by Jessica Tollestrup.

[31] See, for example, "More Than 800,000 Federal Workers Are Furloughed," Wall Street Journal, October 1, 2013. Estimates in this and other media reports were based upon the totals provided by agencies in their contingency plans, available at http://www.whitehouse.gov/omb/contingency-plans. These totals do not include legislative or judicial branch employees.

[32] See, for example, "Pentagon will Order almost All Furloughed Civilian Employees Back to Work." Washington Post, October 5, 2013, and "Agencies Increasingly Calling Back Furloughed Workers," Washington Post, October 10, 2013.

[33] These CRs include H.J.Res. 70, H.J.Res. 71, H.J.Res. 72, H.J.Res. 73, H.J.Res. 75, H.J.Res. 76, H.J.Res. 77, H.J.Res. 79, H.J.Res. 80, H.J.Res. 82, H.J.Res. 83, H.J.Res. 84, H.J.Res. 85, H.J.Res. 89, H.J.Res. 90, H.J.Res. 91, and H.R. 3230.

In: The Government Shutdown of 2013
Editor: Rosanne C. Lundy

ISBN: 978-1-63117-112-3
© 2014 Nova Science Publishers, Inc.

Chapter 5

GOVERNMENT SHUTDOWN: OPERATIONS OF THE DEPARTMENT OF DEFENSE DURING A LAPSE IN APPROPRIATIONS[*]

Amy Belasco and Pat Towell

SUMMARY

Because Congress did not provide any FY2014 funding for the Department of Defense (DOD) by October 1, 2013, the beginning of the new fiscal year, DOD, like other agencies, is now subject to a lapse in appropriations during which agencies are generally required to shut down. The Office of Management and Budget (OMB), however, has identified a number of exceptions to the requirement that agencies cease operations, including a blanket exception for activities that "provide for the national security."

With the approach of the Treasury Department's estimate of an October 17, 2013, deadline for raising the debt ceiling, concerns have grown about the potential effect on government programs and workers. If the Treasury Department were to continue the current practice of paying bills as they come due, DOD programs ranging from payments to military retirees to contractor bills could be delayed or reduced, a situation that differs from the current government shutdown. It is difficult to predict

---

[*] This is an edited, reformatted and augmented version of a Congressional Research Service publication, CRS Report for Congress R41745, prepared for Members and Committees of Congress, from www.crs.gov, dated October 15, 2013.

effects because of the uncertainty about Treasury actions, but payment delays could affect all programs and personnel. Negotiations are currently underway to deal with the upcoming deadline.

Concerns about DOD's implementation of the government shutdown continue. On September 25, 2013, DOD issued guidance and a contingency plan that limited the types of "excepted" activities that would continue to be carried out during a shutdown to military operations, unspecified other operations and national security activities, and those necessary to protect the safety of persons and property. As a result, during the lapse in appropriations, some DOD personnel would be "excepted" from furloughs, including all uniformed military personnel, while others would be furloughed and, thus, not be permitted to work. Those civilian personnel who support "excepted" activities—roughly half of DOD's 750,000 civilians—would continue to report for work while the remainder would be furloughed and not paid. Normally, such "excepted" military and civilian personnel would continue to work but would not be paid until after appropriations are subsequently provided.

With enactment of H.R. 3210, the Pay Our Military Act (POMA), on September 30, 2013, however, many defense personnel will be paid on time, including all active-duty personnel, most civilians, and some contractor personnel. On October 5, 2013, Secretary of Defense Chuck Hagel announced that the language in H.R. 3210 would allow DOD to recall most but not all of its civilian employees to work. In addition to those DOD civilians already designated as "excepted," the Administration interpreted H.R. 3210 as permitting the Secretary to recall (and start to pay) those DOD civilians "whose responsibilities contribute to the morale, well-being, capabilities and readiness of service members." This revision of DOD's Contingency Plan would increase the number of DOD civilians returning to work from roughly 50% to about 95%, according to DOD Comptroller Robert Hale. As the services and DOD components implement this decision, civilians will return to work starting this week, and be paid on time under H.R. 3210.

DOD is continuing to review whether the number of contractor personnel, also covered under H.R. 3210, will be increased. Those defense civilian or contractor personnel who were or remain furloughed would only receive pay for that period if Congress passes legislation to pay furloughed personnel. On October 5, 2013, the House unanimously passed H.R. 3223, which would provide retroactive pay for all federal employees, as occurred during the 1995 to 1996 shutdown. The President has announced his support of the bill. The Senate has not yet taken it up.

On October 10, 2013, in reaction to considerable controversy in Congress, the President signed H.J.Res. 91, Honoring the Families of Fallen Soldiers Act, to provide for payment of death gratuities and other funeral expenses. Both houses had passed the bill unanimously. Previously, the Secretary of Defense had determined that such expenses were not covered under POMA. CBO estimates that the new law would cost about $150 million over the course of a year.

On October 2 and October 3, 2013, the House passed five "mini" Continuing Resolutions (CRs) providing funding for the District of Columbia, NIH, various museums, Veterans Administration disability programs, and pay for non-activated reservists, generally at FY2013 levels including the sequester now in effect. That package includes H.R. 3230, which would expand the number of reservists who would be paid on time from activated reservists (such as those deployed for the Afghan war) who are already covered by H.R. 3210, to non-activated duty reservists who are performing weekend drills. Based on press reports of reactions from the Senate leadership, however, the Senate is not likely to take up the bill.

The authority to continue some activities during a lapse in appropriations is governed by the Antideficiency Act, codified at 31 U.S.C. 1341 and 1342, as interpreted by Department of Justice (DOJ) legal opinions and reflected in Office of Management and Budget (OMB) guidance to executive agencies. Subject to review by OMB, each agency is responsible for making specific determinations on which activities may continue during a shutdown and which may not.

Legally, according to DOJ and OMB guidance, activities that may continue during a lapse in appropriations include (1) activities "necessary to bring about the orderly termination of an agency's functions"; (2) administration of benefit payments provided through funds that remain available in the absence of new appropriations, including, in the case of DOD, military retirement benefits; (3) activities and purchases financed with prior year funds and ongoing activities for which funding has already been obligated; (4) activities undertaken on the basis of constitutional authorities of the President; and (5) activities related to "emergencies involving the safety of human life or the protection of property." The Defense Department attributes its authority to carry on national security-related operations mainly to Section 1342 of the Antideficiency Act, which permits the continuation of activities to protect human life and property.

In addition to military operations, other activities that would continue under a shutdown by virtue of the Anti-Deficiency Act include operation of DOD Dependent Schools, child care centers, and DOD medical activities, including TRICARE services for dependents, but not non-essential services, such as elective surgery in military medical facilities. Passage of POMA considerably broadened the types of support activities, primarily performed by civilians, that would continue during the shutdown. A CBO estimate suggests that POMA appropriated $200 billion, or about one-third or of DOD's $614 billion FY2014 request.

The roughly 5% of DOD's civilians who would continue to be furloughed continue to face a pay gap, potentially imposing hardships on many families, unless legislation providing retroactive pay is enacted. Contracting activities that supported military activities and payments to vendors derived from prior multiyear appropriations could also continue. The status of many contractor personnel remains unclear. While some new contract obligations to support "excepted" activities could be signed, monies could not be disbursed while other new contracts would be delayed. This could create some confusion and, potentially, disruptions to supplies of some material and services, particularly if full funding for DOD is not restored soon.

INTRODUCTION

Because Congress did not provide funding for FY2014, the new fiscal year beginning October 1, 2013, the Department of Defense (DOD), like other agencies, is now subject to a lapse in appropriations.[1] In that event, agencies are generally required to shut down, although the Office of Management and Budget (OMB) has identified a number of exceptions to that rule, including a blanket exception for activities that "provide for the national security."[2] Other than continuing to perform such "excepted" activities, agencies are generally required to terminate operations, and personnel who are not performing "excepted" activities are now furloughed after working only long enough to ensure an orderly shutdown.[3]

On September 25, 2013, Deputy Secretary of Defense Ashton B. Carter issued guidance and a contingency plan to continue essential activities in the event that appropriations lapsed. These activities included not only the war in Afghanistan (including preparing troops to deploy) but also other (unspecified in this guidance) military operations, and "many other operations necessary for safety of human life and protection of property, including operations essential for the security of our Nation." Such activities would be considered "excepted" from furloughs. All other activities would shut down.[4]

Distinctions between a Shutdown and Reaching the Debt Ceiling

In testimony before the Senate Finance Committee on October 10, 2103, Secretary of the Treasury Jacob J. Lew suggested that Treasury believes that the federal government will "run out of borrowing authority" on October 17, 2013, and will have insufficient cash on hand to meet all government obligations "including Social Security and Medicare benefits, payments to our military and veterans, and contracts with private suppliers—for the first time in our history."[5] Under this scenario, DOD benefit programs for military retirement and concurrent receipt could be delayed if the debt ceiling is not raised, which is not the case during the current government shutdown, where payments to military retirees are protected, as are salaries of troops, and DOD civilians after enactment of H.R. 3210, Pay Our Troops Act.

If the debt ceiling is reached, there is some controversy, however, about whether Treasury could make distinctions between one type of payment and another rather than simply paying bills as they come due and are processed. Some have argued that in such a situation the Treasury could prioritize payments in order to avoid a technical default by paying interest due on debt first as part of a policy to choose to make certain types of payments before others. The Treasury argues that it does not have the authority to make such distinctions. In addition, some suggest that making such distinctions would violate the Impoundment Control Act of 1974 as amended, which prohibits deferring particular payments.[6]

In addition to prioritizing payments, Treasury, in 2012, considered but rejected other options, including

- asset sales—as against taxpayer interests;
- across-the-board reductions—as difficult to implement; or,
- the "least harmful" one of delaying payments, which would be "worsened each day ... potentially causing great hardships to millions of Americans and harm to the economy."[7]

It is difficult, if not impossible, to predict potential effects on Department of Defense programs or benefits because of the uncertainties.[8] If payments to defense contractors were delayed, the government could incur interest penalties, and contractors could eventually face liquidity problems. If payments to trust funds (Tricare for Life, military retirement) were delayed and not repaid, the solvency of those funds could be affected. If payments to troops or DOD civilians were delayed, this could be seen as breaking a contractual relationship, as well as harming morale.

Recent Developments in the Shutdown

On September 30, 2013, President Obama signed H.R. 3210, the Pay Our Military Act (POMA), which was passed unanimously earlier in the House and

Senate.[9] This act provides appropriations to cover the *pay and allowances* of all members of the armed forces performing "active service" ("active service" includes both active duty and full-time National Guard duty),[10] and those DOD civilians and contractor personnel whom the Secretary of Defense determines are providing support to these members of the armed forces. This act ensures that those personnel will be paid on time rather than being dependent on passage of a full continuing resolution (CR) or regular appropriations act.[11]

On October 10, 2013, the President signed H.J.Res. 91, which provides for the payment of death gratuities and other funeral expenses for military personnel. Known as the "Honoring the Families of Fallen Soldiers Act," this act was passed in response to considerable controversy in Congress and the press about the Secretary of Defense's determination that these expenses were not covered under the Pay Our Military Act (POMA), passed on September 30, 2012.

According to the Administration's interpretation, the language in POMA providing appropriations to cover "pay and allowances" of active-service personnel did not cover death gratuities, an interpretation questioned by some Members of Congress and some analysts. An October 9, 2013, CRS memo, "Payment of Death Gratuities under the Pay Our Military Act," argues that previous statutory language provides that death gratuity payments are to be made from "payment to members" and that POMA language could be construed to include this type of payment.[12] During a House Armed Services hearing on October 10, 2013, on implementation of POMA, several Members raised concerns about the Department's interpretation.[13]

CBO estimates that H.J.Res. 91 will cost $150 million on an annualized basis.[14] Like POMA, the act is in effect until passage of a regular or continuing appropriations act.

DOD Revises Its Guidance on Furloughing Certain Civilians

On October 5, 2013, Secretary of Defense Chuck Hagel announced that after consultation with the Department of Justice, it was decided that the new law, H.R. 3210, would permit DOD to recall most, but not all, DOD civilians from furlough rather than the fewer number "excepted" from furlough under DOD's original September 25, 2013, Contingency Plan. Under the original plan, only those DOD civilians whose "support activities are felt directly by covered members of the armed forces" (i.e., those performing military operations or required for health and safety) were "excepted" (see *Appendix A*).[15]

The Administration interpreted H.R. 3210 as also permitting the recall of those DOD civilians *"whose responsibilities contribute to the morale, well-being, capabilities and readiness of service members* [italics added]".[16] This revision of DOD's Contingency Plan would increase the number of DOD civilians returning to work from roughly 50% to about 95%, according to DOD Comptroller Robert Hale.[17] Under DOD's revised Contingency Plan reflecting this interpretation of H.R. 3210, DOD civilians are being recalled from furlough if they:

- "contribute support to service members and their families *on an ongoing basis* [italics added]" (such as health care and family support programs, repair and maintenance of weapon systems on bases, training associated with readiness, installation support, commissary, payroll activities, and administrative support); and
- "contribute to capabilities and *sustaining force readiness* and that, if interrupted, would affect service members' ability to *conduct assigned missions in the future* [italics added]" (such as acquisition program management, depot maintenance, intelligence, information technology and other administrative support) (see *Appendix B* for complete text).[18]

The services and defense agencies are currently determining how to carry out the revised guidance. As the services and DOD components implement this decision, civilians will return to work starting this week and will become eligible to be paid on time under H.R. 3210.

Because H.R. 3210 only covers the pay and allowances of personnel, but not "critical parts and supplies" necessary to provide that support, Secretary of Defense Chuck Hagel warned that at some point once current inventories run out, DOD civilians would not be able to do their jobs. At that point, he would be "forced once again to send them home."[19] It is also possible that scheduled two-week annual training for reservists could be delayed if the necessary travel and support are not available.

DOD is continuing to review whether the number of contractor personnel, also covered under H.R. 3210, will be increased. Expanding the number of contractor personnel covered could be problematic because it could be difficult to determine the amount of monies providing pay, the funding covered in POMA. Contracts are typically written in terms of the goods or services to be provided rather than the amount for pay, one element of cost.

The Issue of Retroactive Pay for Civilians

Those defense civilian or contractor personnel who were or remain furloughed would only receive pay for that period if Congress passes legislation to pay furloughed personnel. Civilians recalled under POMA will also not be paid for furloughed time in early October unless Congress chooses to do so.[20] On October 5, 2013, the House unanimously passed H.R. 3223, which would provide retroactive pay for all federal employees, as occurred during the 1995 to 1996 shutdown. The President has announced his support.[21] The Senate has not taken up the bill at this time.

The Issue of Pay for Guard and Reserve Drill Training

On October 3, 2013, the House passed H.R. 3230, Pay Our Guard and Reserve Act, which would provide appropriations to cover the pay of inactive-duty weekend training reservists in FY2014 until a regular or continuing resolution appropriations act is passed.[22] (Reservists performing two-week annual training are already covered under H.R. 3210.) Although reservists would be paid, it is not clear how much training would take place because H.R. 3230 does not provide appropriations to cover related training costs (e.g., fuel, spare parts, food services, and ammunition). Reservists might be confined to training that did not involve additional expenses beyond their pay, although DOD might be able to draw on existing stocks or existing contracts to address these issues at least in the short-term.

This bill is part of a package of five "mini" CRs that would provide funding, generally at the FY2013-enacted level including the effects of sequestration, for the District of Columbia, the National Institutes of Health, various museums, Veterans Administration funding, and pay for guard and reservists. According to press reports, the Senate leadership is not interested in considering partial funding appropriations of particular agencies, and the White House has issued a veto threat.[23]

DOD's Contingency Plan for a Shutdown

In a September 30, 2013, press conference, DOD Comptroller Robert Hale suggested that while all military personnel would continue to report for duty, only those reservists, DOD civilians, and contractor personnel providing support for the Afghanistan war and other unspecified military operations would continue to work. As an example, DOD Comptroller Hale suggested that civilians providing support for some military operations, such as ships deployed in the Mediterranean, would be "excepted," but that civilian personnel supporting other military activities, such as peacetime training off of

Norfolk, would be furloughed. Individual commanding officers are making these decisions. Comptroller Hale agreed that roughly half of DOD's civilian workforce of about 800,000 would be furloughed, as was estimated in 2011 during previous shutdown planning.[24]

In DOD's September 23, 2013, memorandum to all its employees, Deputy Secretary of Defense Ashton B. Carter said that under the department's plan in the event of a funding lapse, while "all military personnel would continue in a normal duty status, a large number of our civilian employees would be temporarily furloughed."[25] Three days later, in a September 26, 2013, memo, the Deputy Secretary said that "commanders and supervisors will ... provide additional detail [and] your status under a potential lapse.[26] For those activities that are not excepted, personnel were expected to come in to carry out "orderly shutdown activities" that are expected to take no more than three or four hours.[27]

Debate over Interpretation of H.R. 3210, "Pay Our Military Act"

Although the President signed H.R. 3210 on September 30, 2013, the Department of Defense did not revise its contingency plan until October 5, 2013, after consulting the Department of Justice. This delay appears to reflect some debate about how to interpret the language in the new law, which provides appropriations to cover the pay and allowances of those DOD employees who are currently "excepted" from furlough, hence paying those personnel on time, and gives the Secretary of Defense authority to bring previously furloughed civilians and contractor personnel back to work, provided he determines that they are providing support to members of the armed forces performing active service. Some argued that this latter group could constitute all or nearly all DOD civilians and contractors.

Initially, Secretary of Defense Hagel indicated that this issue of designating additional groups of civilians or contractors for return from furlough was under review in the Administration. In an October 1, 2013, press conference, Secretary of Defense Chuck Hagel said:

> Our lawyers are now looking through the law that the president signed, along with the Department of Justice lawyers and OMB, to see if there's any margin here or widening in the interpretation of the law regarding exempt versus non-exempt civilians. Our lawyers believe that maybe we can expand the exempt status. We don't know if that's the case, but we are exploring that, so that we could cut back from the furloughs some of the civilians that had to leave.[28]

That same day, Representative Bud P. McKeon, the Chair of the House Armed Services Committee, sent a letter to Secretary Hagel arguing that H.R. 3210 provides the Secretary with "broad latitude" to end the furloughs for DOD civilians.

> I believe the legislation provides you with broad latitude and I encourage you to use it. The text does not limit to provision of pay to civilians who were previously categorized by the Administration as "excepted" or "essential" for the purposes of Department of Defense operations in the event of a government shutdown. Therefore, I strongly encourage you to use the authority Congress has given you to keep national security running, rather than keeping defense civilians at home when they are authorized to work. [29]

The congressional intent of the legislation is not entirely clear.[30] In a recent statement, Representative Mike Coffman, sponsor of H.R. 3210, suggested that H.R. 3210 would protect "the pay for Department of Defense civilian employees and contractors whose work is essential for military operations."[31]

On October 5, 2013, after several days of consultation, the Department of Defense made a determination that H.R. 3210 allowed the department to revise its guidance and recall most of its civilian workforce. The Secretary of Defense has not yet made a determination of whether to revise its guidance about contractor employees (see "DOD Revises Its Guidance on Furloughing Certain Civilians").

Debate over Interpretation of H.R. 3210

The language in Section 2(a)(1) of H.R. 3210 provides appropriations to cover the pay and allowances of all members of the armed forces performing "active service" ("active service" includes both active duty and full-time National Guard duty) during any period in FY2014 in which interim or full-year appropriations are not available. The language in Sections 2(a)(2) and 2(a)(3) provides appropriations to cover the pay and allowances of those DOD civilians and contractor personnel whom the Secretary of Defense determines "are providing support to members of the Armed Forces described in paragraph (1)."

> DOD's September 25, 2013, contingency plan guidance—which is derived from the laws and policies governing operations in the absence of appropriations—makes distinctions between the types of activities for which civilian and contractor personnel would be "excepted" from furlough based on the types of activities being conducted by the military. For example, while all support for the Afghan war would be provided, support for day-to-day peacetime training for active-duty military would not necessarily be conducted.
>
> The debate over H.R. 3210 appears to revolve around the extent to which the authority of the bill should be confined to those civilians and contractors who are already considered "excepted," or whether the Secretary of Defense should apply it more broadly to include additional DOD civilian or contractor personnel.
>
> On October 5, 2013, DOD announced that it was adopting the broader interpretation, and substantially modified its original guidance. The issue of whether to expand the number of contractor personnel remains under review.

QUESTIONS ABOUT DOD OPERATIONS DURING A LAPSE IN FUNDING

The 2013 DOD guidance, like 2011 guidance, provides that many DOD activities would continue during the period of a funding lapse, though other activities would halt. Some personnel would be "excepted" from furloughs, including all uniformed military personnel on active duty, while others would be subject to furlough. "Excepted" military, reservists, and civilian personnel who would continue to work during a lapse in appropriations would be paid on time because of the passage of H.R. 3210. Other furloughed personnel would not be paid, and may be paid retroactively if Congress chooses to do so once annual appropriations are enacted. This report provides an overview of recent guidance and precedents over the past 30 years that have governed planning for DOD operations in the event of a funding lapse, and it discusses their implications for a shutdown.

Among the questions addressed are

- the effects of a shutdown on pay for uniformed military personnel and DOD civilians;

- how reservists and military technicians may be affected;
- types of activities to protect persons and property that are "excepted;"
- potential effects on contracting;
- whether DOD Dependent Schools or childcare centers would continue to operate during a shutdown;
- how long operations of the Defense Finance and Accounting Service could continue; and
- whether the "Feed and Forage Act," 41 U.S.C. 11, which allows the Defense Department to obligate funds in advance of appropriations for certain purposes, might be invoked to provide additional flexibility during a funding lapse.

Answers to some of these questions are quite simple, others complex, and others uncertain.

Assuming that past Attorney General, OMB guidance, recent DOD guidance, and current new law are followed in the event of a shutdown, brief answers to these questions are as follows:

- *Pay of Uniformed Military Personnel and DOD Civilians:* The current DOD guidance provides that all active-duty military personnel would be "excepted" from furloughs during a lapse in funding, as they have been in the past.[32] H.R. 3210, the Pay Our Military Act, signed by President Obama on September 30, 2013, provides appropriations to allow the Defense Department to cover the pay and allowances of members of the armed forces performing active service, and the DOD civilians and contractors who provide support to them. H.R. 3210 provides this authority through January 1, 2015, or until other regular or continuing appropriations are enacted.[33] This bill means that today's experience differs from the previous government shutdown in 1995 and 1996, when this authority was not provided and DOD was marginally affected by the first short shutdown and not by the second, longer shutdown because a defense appropriations bill had been enacted.
- *Potential effects on reservists:* DOD's Contingency Plan specifies that activated reservists, like active-duty military, would continue to conduct their duties. The Contingency Plan also specifies that reservists will not perform inactive duty training (e.g., weekend drills) "except where such training directly supports an excepted activity" and may not be ordered to

active duty (e.g., for annual training) "except in support of those military operations and activities necessary for national security, including fulfilling associated pre-deployment requirements."[34] This would include those reservists currently "training up" for deployments. H.R. 3210 provides appropriations to cover the pay and allowances of activated reservists, but would not cover the compensation of any reservists performing inactive duty training. Under DOD's Contingency Plan, military technicians—who are federal civilian employees required to hold membership in the reserves as a condition of their civilian employment—will continue to perform their civilian duties only if they are deemed necessary to carry out excepted activities.

- *National Security and Protection of Life and Property*: The 2013 DOD guidance includes not only military operations in Afghanistan but also some training and other support necessary for the Afghan war or other military operations. Excepted military activities are those considered necessary to "execute planned or contingency operations necessary for national security," including "administrative, logistical, medical, and other activities in direct support of such activities." Other military activities deemed necessary to carry out those operations are recruiting during contingency operations, command, control, communications, computer, intelligence, surveillance and reconnaissance. Not listed are depot maintenance repair of equipment or base support, activities which typically do not involve active-duty personnel.[35] Presumably, civilians performing activities *not* directly required to support military operations would be furloughed under DOD's original plan. This plan was modified with new guidance issued after enactment of H.R. 3210 (see "Recent Developments").

- *Contractor Activities:* Contracts that rely on previously appropriated funds, whether for weapon systems with deliveries over several years or support services where contracts may span fiscal years, would continue. The Defense Department, however, would only be able to sign new contracts for goods funded with FY2014 funds for activities deemed necessary to support military operations, and no monies could be disbursed (checks sent out) under those contracts. An exception could be any contractor personnel covered by H.R. 3210, whose support was necessary for military operations, such as contractor personnel in Afghanistan.[36]

- *Operation of DOD Dependent Schools and Childcare:* The 2013 and 2001 DOD guidance provides that, the support that dependent schools provide to military personnel is directly enough related to national security that the schools may continue to operate during a shutdown.[37] The 2013 guidance also concludes that child care "essential to readiness" may continue as well as emergency family support.[38]
- *Operation of the Defense Finance and Accounting Service (DFAS) and Other Working Capital Funds:* Some DFAS operations would be likely to continue through a funding lapse, initially using funds drawn from reimbursements from prior year funds, and then to issue paychecks for those covered under H.R. 3210 (see "Recent Developments"), and to control funds for contracts in support of excepted activities.[39] DFAS personnel needed to administer military retired pay and other retiree benefits would be expected to work during a funding lapse because the authority to distribute benefits drawn from multi-year funds, including retirement funds, is implied by the responsibility agencies have to provide payments to which recipients are entitled.[40] Military pensions and other retirement benefits are entitlements financed through the military retirement and health care fund, which is available independently of annual defense appropriations.
- Though new appropriations are not available during a funding lapse, a substantial amount of money provided to the Defense Department is available for obligation for more than one year, including funding for R&D, procurement, military construction, and purchases of material for inventories of stock funds. The 2013 shutdown guidance provides that DFAS can make adjustments for prior year unobligated balances, suggesting that some administration, contract oversight, and auditing functions, some of which are carried out by DFAS, may also continue.
- Many DFAS personnel are paid through reimbursements from other appropriated accounts for services that DFAS provides to organizations within DOD, and those funds could be available to support DFAS services to continue national security-related operations.[41] DOD's 2013 guidance provides that other activities funded through reimbursements would also continue operations as long as cash was available, recently estimated as about two weeks, according to DOD Comptroller Robert Hale.[42]
- *Authority to Obligate Funds Under the "Feed and Forage Act":* The Feed and Forage Act, 41 U.S.C. 11, says, in part,

No contract or purchase on behalf of the United States shall be made, unless the same is authorized by law or is under an appropriation adequate to its fulfillment, except in the Department of Defense and ... the Coast Guard when it is not operating as a service in the Navy for clothing, subsistence, forage, fuel, quarters, transportation, or medical and hospital supplies.

During the Vietnam War, the law was used to provide funds when supplemental appropriations were delayed. In more recent years, it has been used mainly to provide short-term funding for unplanned military operations. If invoked during a funding lapse, the act would give DOD authority to obligate funds in advance of appropriations for the limited number of purposes specified. While the DOD 2013 guidance mentions the Feed and Forage Act, use of the Feed and Forage Act during a funding lapse appears unnecessary during earlier shutdowns, Attorney General and OMB guidance has allowed national security-related operations to continue. The authority for DOD to continue national security-related activities appears to be considerably broader than that provided by the Feed and Forage Act, which is limited in purpose and which does not directly provide authority to obligate funds for pay of military personnel.[43] Moreover, like the authority provided by the Antideficiency Act, the Feed and Forage Act permits only the obligation of funds and not disbursements until funds are subsequently appropriated—neither law allows the Defense Department to issue pay checks or to make other payments.[44] While invocation of the Feed and Forage Act during a shutdown is conceivable, it is not clear what purpose it would serve.[45]

- *Activities to Protect Health and Safety*: The 2013 DOD guidance includes a broad range of activities under the "safety of persons and protection of property" category. These activities range from emergency response and intelligence support to terrorist threat warnings to emergency repair of utilities and associated equipment, and some counterdrug activities.[46]

IMPLICATIONS OF DOD GUIDANCE

The legal authority for critical military operations to continue is reasonably clear. The 2013 guidance also provides that all other activities needed, in the view of DOD, to support these "excepted" activities, may carry on, including logistics, intelligence, communications, and contracting functions. Guidance also defines quite broadly the range of activities that are permitted to continue in support of operational forces, including personnel support activities such as defense dependent schools and child care, temporary duty travel in support of exempted activities, and new contracts for exempted activities. The Administration is free to change these guidelines, based on its own interpretation of relevant laws and regulations.

Nonetheless, though authority to sustain ongoing military operations is clear in principle, a lapse in appropriations, if it were to extend for more than a very limited period of time, could disrupt operations to some degree. As the DOD guidance illustrates, efforts to distinguish between, on the one hand, those activities that are sufficiently important for national security to warrant continuation during a lapse in appropriations and, on the other hand, activities that do not directly support national security involve difficult, and to some degree, arbitrary judgments.

Unit training would continue for some combat units, but not for others, depending on their place in deployment or force generation plans. For example, military personnel preparing to deploy to Afghanistan would continue. Medical personnel would continue to provide services to active duty personnel, but not to dependents or retirees who might normally receive non-emergency services in the same facilities. Issuance of some contracts would continue during a shutdown, but other contracting activity, perhaps done by the same people, would not. Local commanders would have the authority to make final judgments on which activities and missions are essential and must be supported; this could result in inconsistent decisions on what activities may continue and what must be shut down across the whole force.

Effects on Military, Civilian, and Contractor Personnel

Virtually all military personnel and most civilians are normally paid out of annual appropriations. With passage of H.R. 3210, funds for all active-duty military, activated reservists, and those DOD civilian and contractor personnel whose support is necessary for military operations, for other DOD "excepted" activities, and to support active service personnel will be paid on time despite the lapse in other appropriations. Other DOD civilian and contractor personnel would not be paid. DOD is continuing to review the status of many contractor personnel under H.R. 3210.

Reservists performing weekend drills would not report for duty or be paid under DOD guidance unless Congress decides otherwise at a later time. Furloughed personnel could be subject to financial hardships if a lapse in appropriations extends past a normal pay date, since no disbursements may be made. The hardships that a sudden stop in pay would impose on civilian or contractor personnel, would, of course, vary depending on individual circumstances. Families with a second income and with substantial savings might be able to manage with few problems. Others, particularly those with young families and limited savings, might be affected very badly.

Effects of Limits on Expenditures on Contracting

In the event of a lapse in funding, the Defense Department would have the authority to obligate funds for goods and services needed to sustain its continuing operations—that is, it can sign contracts with a binding commitment to pay providers—for activities deemed essential to support military operations, but the Antideficiency Act prohibits expenditures or issuing checks for amounts obligated in advance of appropriations. While contracts for activities necessary to support military operations could be signed, reimbursements could not be provided and it is not clear that all vendors would be willing to provide goods or services under these circumstances, particularly if a shutdown appears likely to continue for an extended period.

Other new contracts, for example, for new weapon system programs or for higher production rates could be delayed until FY2014 appropriations are enacted if the connection to ongoing military operations is indirect. There is also likely to be some confusion among contractors because funds remaining available from prior years can continue to be distributed, but not new funds. In DOD appropriations acts, funding for R&D is typically available for obligation for two years, for most procurement for three years, and for shipbuilding for five years. Contract authority to purchase stocks of material for inventories is not limited by fiscal year. Unobligated balances of funds for those purposes would remain available even in the absence of new funding.

Money for operation and maintenance, however, is generally available for obligation for only one year, so most funding for day-to-day operations of the department would lapse and operations could continue only under the Antideficiency Act exceptions that allow the obligation of funds, but not disbursements. Whether vendors could be paid, therefore, depends on which pot of money obligations are made from, and money for more immediate, readiness-related activities would generally not be used to make prompt payments.

Under the circumstances, the Defense Department can be expected to sustain its most important operations, but not without some difficulties in managing the acquisition of material and services from vendors.

AUTHORITIES AND CONDITIONS AFFECTING DOD OPERATIONS IN THE ABSENCE OF APPROPRIATIONS

Based on the 2013 guidance, as well as earlier precedents followed over the past 30 years, the Department of Defense may continue, in the absence of appropriations, to carry on a quite broad range of activities. The most far-reaching authority that affects DOD is authority to continue activities that "provide for the national security."[47]

Even DOD's authority to provide for national security, however, may be constrained by legal limits on the financial procedures that are permitted when appropriations lapse. Among other things, in order to carry on activities that are permitted to continue, but for which appropriations have lapsed, funds may be obligated in advance of appropriations (i.e., legally binding contractual commitments may be made), but expenditures of funds that derive from such obligations (i.e., the payment of bills with checks or electronic remittances) are prohibited. As a result, though uniformed military personnel and many DOD civilian employees may be expected to continue in their duties during a funding lapse, those normally paid with current-year appropriated funds, including virtually all uniformed personnel and most civilians, will not receive pay until after appropriations become available. Nor will payments to vendors for goods and services be permitted if the payments derive from contracts entered into in advance of appropriations.

The legal authority under which the Department of Defense may continue operations in the event of a funding lapse is established by the Antideficiency Act, now codified at 31 U.S.C. 1341 and 1342. The legal interpretation of the conditions under which operations may continue has been established, in turn, by Department of Justice legal opinions and Office of Management and Budget directives issued initially in 1980 and 1981, and that OMB has referred to in providing guidance on shutdowns since then. Agencies, including DOD, have also been required to prepare detailed plans for implementing a shutdown when lapses in appropriations were anticipated.

Ultimately, federal agency plans, based on OMB guidance, determine which activities will continue in the event of a shutdown and which will not. Current agency plans are now posted on OMB's website or by individual agencies. DOD operations in the event of a shutdown would also be governed by financial management procedures that would, in turn, affect how a shutdown is managed.

Key Department of Justice and OMB Guidance on Operations During a Lapse in Appropriations[48]

- An opinion by Attorney General Benjamin Civiletti on April 25, 1980, that found few exceptions to Antideficiency Act limits on funding in the absence of appropriations;
- A memorandum by OMB Director James McIntyre on August 28, 1980, that required agencies to submit plans for operations in the event of a lapse in appropriations;
- A memorandum by OMB Director James McIntyre on September 30, 1980, that provided guidance to agencies on operations permitted to continue during a lapse in appropriations;
- An extensive opinion by Attorney General Civiletti on January 16, 1981, reviewing in detail the legal basis for the guidance that OMB provided on September 30, 1980;
- A memorandum by OMB Director Richard Darman on November 17, 1981, that repeated the guidance provided by the September 30, 1980, OMB memorandum and that added some further guidance, including the point that obligations of funds may be permitted in advance of appropriations, but not expenditures;
- A memorandum by Assistant Attorney General Walter Dellinger on August 16, 1995, addressed to OMB Director Alice Rivlin, that found that a 1990 amendment to the Antideficiency Act provided no basis for altering earlier guidance on agency operations in the event of a lapse in appropriations;
- A memorandum to the heads of executive departments and agencies by OMB Director Rivlin on August 22, 1995, that conveyed the Dellinger memorandum and that required agencies to maintain contingency plans for a lapse in appropriations based on the September 30, 1980, and November 17, 1981, OMB memoranda;

- A memorandum for the heads of executive departments and agencies by OMB Director Lew on April 7, 2011, providing further guidance on contracting, grand administration, and payments processing during a lapse in appropriations;
- A memorandum for the heads of executive departments and agencies by OMB Director Burwell on September 17, 2013, providing further guidance on contracting, grand administration, and payments processing during a lapse in appropriations.

The following discussion (1) briefly reviews the legal basis for the Department of Defense to continue operations during a funding lapse and the attendant legal constraints on the scope of activities and the financial mechanisms that are permitted; (2) provides a brief overview of the possible impact of a lapse in funding on military and civilian personnel, on current military operations including operations in Afghanistan, and on day-to-day business operations of the Department of Defense; and (3) provides selected excerpts from DOD guidance on activities that may continue during a funding lapse and those that may not.

THE ANTIDEFICIENCY ACT

The Antideficiency Act, now codified at 31 U.S.C. 1341 and 1342,[49] generally prohibits the obligation or expenditure of funds exceeding amounts appropriated. It provides two quite broad exceptions, however:

- Section 1341 says that an employee of the United States Government may not "involve [the] government in a contract or obligation for the payment of money before an appropriation is made unless authorized by law." Subsequent Attorney General Opinions on operations permitted during a lapse in appropriations have been intended, in part, to identify what obligations in advance of appropriations should be considered to be "authorized by law."
- Section 1342 says, in part, that "An officer or employee of the United States Government may not accept voluntary services ... or employ personal services exceeding that authorized by law except for emergencies involving the safety of human life or the protection of property." One basis for Department of Defense operations to continue during a funding lapse is this authority to employ personnel

to protect human life and property. Department of Justice opinions have found that the authority to employ personal services implies the authority to procure material that personnel may need to carry out their emergency responsibilities (see below for a discussion). OMB guidance to agencies on preparations for a shutdown has identified a quite extensive range of activities that are permitted to continue in the absence of appropriations in order to protect human life and property.

While the Antideficiency Act permits certain exceptions to the requirement that agency operations cease when appropriations are not provided, the exceptions permit only the obligation of funds in advance of appropriations for the excepted activities, not the expenditure of funds. Contracts for material and services may be signed, and personnel may continue to be employed, but the Antideficiency Act does not permit agencies to make payments to vendors or issue pay checks to personnel if the payments would have to be drawn from amounts obligated in advance of appropriations. To be absolutely clear, no money is actually available, but only the promise to provide funds at some time in the future.

OMB AND JUSTICE DEPARTMENT GUIDANCE ON DOD ACTIVITIES PERMITTED DURING A LAPSE IN APPROPRIATIONS

Attorney General opinions released in April 1980 and January 1981 and OMB memoranda issued in September 1980 and November 1981—and referred to repeatedly in later years—provide the basic guidance on activities that DOD and other executive branch agencies may be allowed to continue when appropriations are not provided. In general, these activities are understood to be "authorized by law" under Section 1341 of the Antideficiency Act or to permit the employment of personal services for emergencies involving the safety of human life or the protection of property under Section 1342. The principal activities that the Justice Department and OMB have determined may continue include the following.

- *Activities "necessary to bring about the orderly termination of an agency's functions":* The Attorney General found that agencies may obligate funds to shut down operations after a funding lapse under the terms of the Antideficiency Act itself, since "it would be impossible in fact for agency heads to terminate all agency functions without incurring any obligations whatsoever in advance of appropriations." In general, such activities are expected to be very limited— OMB guidance in 2013 said that "orderly shutdown activities should take no more than three or four hours following the expiration of funding."[50]

- *Administration of benefit payments provided through funds that remain available in the absence of new appropriations:* The Attorney General found that departments are "authorized to incur obligations in advance of appropriations for the administration of benefit payments under entitlement programs when the funds for the payments themselves are not subject to a one-year appropriation." This follows, he said, from the premise that funding is "authorized by necessary implication from the specific terms of duties that have been imposed on, or authorities that have been invested in, the agency." The Social Security Administration, by this reasoning, may continue to pay personnel and to fund operations needed to manage pensions during a lapse in funding because of its responsibility to distribute benefits that are provided through a permanent trust fund that is not affected by a lapse in appropriations. Presumably, DOD administration of military retired pay and medical benefits may continue as well.

- *Activities and purchases financed with prior year funds and ongoing activities for which funding has already been obligated:* Substantial amounts of DOD funding are provided in accounts that are available for obligation for more than a year—R&D funding is typically available for two years, most procurement for three years, and shipbuilding funds for five years. Contract authority to procure material for stockpiles is also available as "no year" money. Contract authority provided understanding law and unobligated balances in the acquisition accounts remain available during a lapse in funding because they have previously been provided—only current-year funding is affected by a lapse in appropriations. Similarly, contracts which have already been signed, and which may require delivery of services or material as ordered, remain valid.[51] Most significantly, obligations already made or new obligations made from funds appropriated in prior years may lead to expenditures of funds, in contrast to obligations made in advance of appropriations. Whether vendors may be paid during the period of a funding lapse, therefore, depends on which pot of money the funds are drawn from—some contractors may be paid as usual while others may not be. At the very least, a degree of confusion is likely. A further complicating factor is whether administrative personnel needed to manage contracts are permitted to continue working. To the extent that acquisition personnel are paid with annual appropriations—which is generally the case— personnel may be available to manage contracts only if they are excepted from a shutdown. It is not necessarily to be assumed that agencies have authority under the Antideficiency Act to except from furloughs personnel needed to administer the use of funds available from prior year appropriations or other sources. Both the 2011 and 2013 DOD guidance, however, say that personnel may continue to administer activities financed with prior year or other available funds that are necessary to support excepted activities.

- *Activities undertaken on the basis of constitutional authorities of the President:* The Attorney General found that the President has an inherent constitutional authority to obligate funds in advance of appropriations to carry out "not only functions that are authorized by statute, but functions authorized by the Constitution as well." When the Constitution grants a specific power to the President, the Attorney General reasoned, "Manifestly, Congress could not deprive the President of this power by purporting to deny him the minimum obligational authority sufficient to carry this power into effect." This does not mean that the President can "legislate his own obligational authorities." But in the opinion of the Attorney General, "the policy objective of the Antideficiency Act ... should not alone be regarded as dispositive of the question of authority." The Attorney General did not specifically address whether this provides a basis for the President to direct that funds be obligated in advance of appropriations for reasons of national security. OMB memoranda since 1980 repeat the conclusion that funding may be continued to "Provide for the national security, including the conduct of foreign relations essential to the national security or the safety of life or property."[52] This wording might be read to imply that the authority of agencies to continue operations related to national security is independent of the authority to continue activities related to the safety of life or the protection of property. National security-related activities may, then, be among those for which obligations in advance of appropriations are considered to be "authorized by law" under Section 1341 of the Antideficiency Act and are permitted independently of Section 1342 and whether or not they protect life or property. For its part, however, the Defense Department has generally not cited any authority beyond that provided in Section 1342.

- Activities that protect life and property: OMB guidance periodically issued in preparation for a shutdown concludes that agencies have the authority to "Conduct essential activities to the extent that they protect life and property."53 The guidance reflects Section 1342 of the Antideficiency Act. Section 1342, however, directly permits the obligation of funds only for employment of "personal services" and not for other purposes. Rather than accept such a limited view of what is permitted, the January 16, 1981, Attorney General opinion provided a basis for expanding the scope of activities permitted under Section 1342 to include the acquisition of material needed to respond to emergencies to those:

> in which a government agency may employ personal services ... it may also ... incur obligations in advance of appropriations for material to enable the employees involved to meet the emergency successfully. In order to effectuate the legislative intent that underlies a statute, it is ordinarily inferred that a statute "carries with it all means necessary and proper to carry out properly the purposes of the law."

OMB memoranda provide a fairly long list of examples of activities permitted to continue on the grounds they protect life and property, including inpatient and emergency outpatient medical care; public health and safety activities; air traffic control; border protection; care of prisoners; law enforcement; disaster assistance; preservation of the banking system; borrowing and tax collection; power production and distribution; and protection of research property. The "protection of property" exception in itself appears to provide the basis for a quite wide range of government activities to continue.

APPENDIX A. 2013 DOD GUIDANCE ON OPERATIONS DURING A LAPSE OF APPROPRIATIONS

Below are excerpts (in italics) from the September 25, 2013, guidance issued by Deputy Secretary of Defense Ashton B. Carter, "Guidance for Continuation of Operations in the Absence of Available Appropriations."

General guidance is followed by a specific list of excepted activities in an attachment.[54]

Excerpts from Memorandum

The Department will, of course, continue to prosecute the war in Afghanistan, including preparation of forces for deployment into that conflict. The Department must, as well, continue many other operations necessary for the safety of human life and protection of property, including operations essential for the security of our nation. These activities will be "excepted" from cessation; all other activities would need to be shut down in an orderly and deliberate fashion, including—with few exceptions—the cessation of temporary duty travel.

All military personnel will continue in a normal duty status regardless of their affiliation with excepted or non-excepted activities. Military personnel will serve without pay until such time as Congress makes appropriated funds available to compensate them for this period of service. Civilian personnel who are engaged in excepted activities will also continue in normal duty status and also will not be paid until Congress makes appropriated funds available. Civilian employees not engaged in excepted activities will be furloughed, i.e., placed in a non-work, non-pay status.

The responsibility for determining which functions would be excepted from shut down resides with the Military Department Secretaries and Heads of DOD Components, who may delegate this authority as they deem appropriate. The attached guidance should be used to assist in making this excepted determination. The guidance does not identify every excepted activity, but rather provides overarching direction and general principles for making these determinations. It should be applied prudently in the context of a Department at war, with decisions guaranteeing our continued robust support for those engaged in that war, and with assurance that the lives and property of our Nation's citizens will be protected.

Excerpts from Attachment: Examples of "Excepted" Activities

Following are excerpts (in italics) from the 2013 DOD shutdown planning guidance which, although not comprehensive, provides in more detail illustrative examples of the types of DOD activities that would and would not be excepted, in case of a lapse of appropriation.

The information provided in this document is not exhaustive, but rather illustrative, and is intended primarily to assist in the identification of those activities that may be continued notwithstanding the absence of available funding authority in the applicable appropriations (excepted activities). Activities that are determined not to be excepted, and which cannot be performed by utilizing military personnel in place of furloughed civilian personnel, will be suspended when appropriated funds expire. The Secretary of Defense may, at any time, determine that additional activities shall be treated as excepted.

Military Personnel

Military personnel are not subject to furlough. Accordingly, military personnel on active duty, including reserve component personnel on Federal active duty, will continue to report for duty and carry out assigned duties. In addition to carrying out excepted activities, military personnel on active duty may be assigned to carry out non-excepted activities, in place of furloughed civilian personnel, to the extent that the non-excepted activity is capable of performance without incurring new obligations.

Reserve component personnel performing Active Guard Reserve (AGR) duty will continue to report for duty to carry out AGR authorized duties. Reserve component personnel will not perform inactive duty training resulting in the obligation of funds, except where such training directly supports an excepted activity, and may not be ordered to active duty, except in support of those military operations and activities necessary for national security listed in Attachment 2, including fulfilling associated pre-deployment requirements. Orders for members of the National Guard currently performing duties under 32 U.S.C. 502(f) will be terminated unless such duties are in support of excepted activities approved by the Secretary of Defense.

Civilian Personnel

Civilian personnel, including military technicians, who are not necessary to carry out or support excepted activities, are to be furloughed. Only the minimum number of civilian employees necessary to carry out excepted activities will be exempt from furlough. Positions that provide direct support to excepted positions may also be deemed excepted if they are critical to performing the excepted activity. Determinations regarding the status of civilian positions will be made on a position by position basis, using the guidance in this document. Determinations shall be made for all positions, including those in the Senior Executive Service or equivalent, as well as those located overseas.

Following the expiration of appropriations, a minimum number of civilian employees may be retained as needed to execute an orderly suspension of non-excepted activities within a reasonable timeframe.

Civilian personnel whose salaries are paid with expired appropriations and later reimbursed from a non-DOD source (e.g., the Foreign Military Sales Trust Fund) are not exempt from furlough solely on that basis. Personnel whose salaries are paid from a DOD appropriation or fund that has sufficient funding authority (e.g., multiyear appropriations with available balances from prior years) will not be subject to furlough. Heads of activities may, on their authority, require the return to work of civilian personnel in the event of developments (natural disasters, accidents, etc.) that pose an imminent danger to life or property.

Contracts

Contractors performing under a contract that was fully obligated upon contract execution (or renewal) prior to the expiration of appropriations may continue to provide contract services, whether in support of excepted activities or not. However, new contracts (including contract renewals or extensions, issuance of task orders, exercise of options) may not be executed unless the contractor is supporting an excepted activity. No funds will be available to pay such new contractors until Congress appropriates additional funds. The expiration of an appropriation does not require the termination of contracts (or issuance of stop work orders) funded by that appropriation unless a new obligation of funds is required under the contract and the contract is not required to support an excepted activity. In cases where new obligation is required and the contract is not required to support an excepted activity, the issuance of a stop work order or the termination of the contract will be required.

The Department may continue to enter into new contracts, or place task orders under existing contracts, to obtain supplies and services necessary to carry out or support excepted activities even though there are no available appropriations. It is emphasized that this authority is to be exercised only when determined to be necessary -where delay in contracting would endanger national security or create a risk to human life or property.

Additionally, when authorized by the Secretary of Defense, contracts for covered items may be entered into under the authority of the Feed and Forage Act.

Protection of Life and Property/National Security[55]

- Military operations and activities authorized by deployment or execute orders, or otherwise approved by the Secretary of Defense, and determined to be necessary for national security, including administrative, logistical, medical, and other activities in direct support of such operations and activities; training and exercises required to prepare for and carry out such operations.
- Activities of forces assigned or apportioned to combatant commands to execute planned or contingent operations necessary for national security, including necessary administrative, logistical, medical, and other activities in direct support of such operations; training and exercises required to prepare for and carry out such operations.
- Activities necessary to continue recruiting for entry into the Armed Forces during contingency operations (as such term is defined in 10 U.S.C 101(13)), including activities necessary to operate Military Entrance Processing Stations (MEPS) and to conduct basic and other training necessary to qualify such recruited personnel to perform their assigned duties.
- Command, control, communications, computer, intelligence, surveillance, and reconnaissance activities required to support national or military requirements necessary for national security or to support other excepted activities, including telecommunications centers and phone switches on installations, and secure conference capability at military command centers.
- Activities required to operate, maintain, assess, and disseminate the collection of intelligence data necessary to support tactical and strategic indications and warning systems, and military operational requirements. Activities necessary to carry out or enforce treaties and other international obligations.

Safety of Persons and Protection of Property

- Response to emergencies, including fire protection, physical and personnel security, law enforcement/counter terrorism, intelligence support to terrorist threat warnings, Explosive Ordnance Disposal

operations, emergency salvage, sub-safe program, nuclear reactor safety and security, nuclear weapons, air traffic control and harbor control, search and rescue, utilities, housing and food services for military personnel, and trash removal.
- *Emergency repair & non-deferrable maintenance to utilities, power distribution system buildings or other real property, including bachelor enlisted quarters (BEQ), bachelor officers' quarters (BOQ), and housing for military personnel.*
- *Repair of equipment needed to support services for excepted activities, including fire trucks, medical emergency vehicles, police vehicles, or material handling vehicles.*
- *Monitoring and maintaining alarms and control systems, utilities, and emergency services.*
- *Receipt/safekeeping of material delivered during shutdown.*
- *Control of hazardous material and monitoring of existing environmental remediation.*
- *Oil spill/hazardous waste cleanup, environmental remediation, and pest control, only to the extent necessary to prevent imminent danger to life or property.*[56]
- *Safe storage or transportation of hazardous materials, including ammunition, chemical munitions, photo processing operations.*
- *Emergency reporting response and input to the National Response Team and coordinating with Environmental Protection Agency (EPA) and other agencies on fire, safety, occupational health, environmental, explosive safety for vector borne disease management.*
- *Activities, both in the Continental United States (CONUS) and overseas, required for the safety of DOD or other U.S. Government employees or for the protection of DOD or other U.S. Government property.*
- *Defense support to civil authorities in response to disasters or other imminent threats to life and property, including activities of the U.S. Army Corps of Engineers with respect to responsibilities to state and local governments that involve imminent threats to life or property.*
- *Foreign humanitarian assistance in response to disaster or other crises posing an imminent threat to life.*
- *Emergency counseling and crisis intervention intake screening and referral services. Suicide and substance abuse counseling.*

- *Counterdrug activities determined to be necessary for the protection of life or property.*
- *Operation of mortuary affairs activities and attendant other services necessary to properly care for the fallen and their families.*
- *Other activities authorized by the Secretary of Defense to provide for the safety of life or protection of property.*

Medical and Dental Care[57]

- *Inpatient care in DOD Medical Treatment Facilities and attendant maintenance of patient medical records.[58]*
- *Acute and emergency outpatient care in DOD medical and dental facilities.*
- *Private Sector Care under TRICARE.*
- *Certification of eligibility for health care benefits.*
- *Veterinary Services that support excepted activities (i.e., food supply and service inspections).*

Acquisition and Logistic Support

- *Contracting, contract administration, and logistics operations in support of excepted activities.*
- *Activities required to contract for and to distribute items as authorized by the Feed and Forage Act (e.g., clothing, subsistence, forage, fuel, quarters, transportation, and medical and hospital supplies).*
- *Central receiving points for storage of supplies and materials purchased prior to the shutdown.*

Education and Training[59]

- Education and training necessary to participate in or support excepted activities.
- DOD Education Activity (DODEA) educational activities.[60]

Legal Activities

- *Litigation activities associated with imminent or ongoing legal action, in forums inside or outside of 000, to the extent required by law or necessary to support excepted activities.*

- *Legal support for excepted activities, including legal assistance for military and civilian employees deployed, or preparing to deploy, in support of military or stability operations.*
- *Legal activities needed to address external (non-judicial) deadlines imposed by non-DOD enforcement agencies, to the extent necessary to continue excepted activities.*

Audit and Investigation Community
- *Criminal investigations related to the protection of life or property, including national security, as determined by the head of the investigating unit, and investigations involving undercover activities.*
- *Counterterrorism and counterintelligence investigations.*

Morale, Welfare and Recreation/Non-appropriated Funds
- *Morale, Welfare, and Recreation (MWR) and Non-Appropriated Fund (NAF) activities necessary to support excepted activities, e.g., operation of mess halls; physical training; child care activities required for readiness.[61]*

Financial Management
- *Activities necessary to control funds, record new obligations incurred in the performance of excepted activities, and manage working capital funds.[62]*
- *Activities necessary to effect upward adjustment of obligations and the reallocation of prior-year unobligated funds in support of excepted activities.*

Working Capital Fund/Revolving Fund[63]
- *Defense Working Capital Fund (DWCF)/ Revolving Fund (RF) activities with positive cash balances may continue to operate until cash reserves are exhausted.*
- *When cash reserves are exhausted, DWCF/RF activities must continue operations in direct support of excepted activities.*

DWCF/RF activities may continue to accept orders financed with appropriations enacted prior to the current fiscal year or unfunded orders from excepted organizations. Unfunded orders will be posted to accounts receivable and not actually billed until appropriations are enacted.

APPENDIX B. DOD, "GUIDANCE FOR IMPLEMENTATION OF PAY OUR MILITARY ACT," OCTOBER 5, 2013

See below for complete text of DOD guidance to reflect the Administration's interpretation of the effects of H.R. 3210, Pay Our Military Act, identifying the number and categories of DOD civilians to be recalled from furlough.[64]

SUBJECT: Guidance for Implementation of Pay Our Military Act

Appropriations provided under the Consolidated and Further Continuing Appropriations Act, 2013 (P.L. 113-6) expired at midnight on Monday, September 30, 2013. Hours before that occurred, the Congress passed and the President signed the Pay Our Military Act. That Act provides appropriations for specified purposes while interim or full-year appropriations for fiscal year 2014 are not in effect, as is currently the case.

First, the Act appropriated such sums as are necessary to provide pay and allowances to members of the Armed Forces, "including reserve components thereof, who perform active service during such period[.]" This provision provides the Department with the funds necessary to pay our military members (including Reserve Component members) on active duty or full-time National Guard duty under Title 32, U.S. Code.

Second, the Act appropriated such sums as are necessary to provide pay and allowances to contractors of DoD who the Secretary determines are providing support to members of the Armed Forces in active service. The Department's lawyers are analyzing what authority is provided by this provision.

Third, the Act appropriated such sums as are necessary to provide pay and allowances to the civilian personnel of the Department of Defense "whom the Secretary ... determines are providing support to members of the Armed Forces" performing active service during such period. The term "pay and allowances" includes annual leave and sick leave.

This Memorandum provides instructions for identifying those civilian personnel within the Department who "are providing support to members of the Armed Forces" within the meaning of the Act. The responsibility for determining which employees fall within the scope of this statute resides with the Military Department Secretaries and Heads of other DoD Components, who may delegate this authority in writing. This guidance must be used in identifying these employees. The guidance does not identify every activity performed by DoD's large civilian workforce, but rather it provides overarching direction and general principles for making these determinations. It should be applied prudently, and in a manner that promotes consistency across the Department.

The Department of Defense consulted closely with the Department of Justice, which expressed its view that the law does not permit a blanket recall of all civilians. Under our current reading of the law, the standard of "support to members of the Armed Forces" requires a focus on those employees whose responsibilities contribute to the morale, well-being, capabilities, and readiness of covered military members during the lapse of appropriations. I have determined that this standard includes all those who are performing activities deemed "excepted" pursuant to the "CONTINGENCY PLAN GUIDANCE FOR CONTINUATION OF ESSENTIAL OPERATIONS IN THE ABSENCE OF AVAILABLE APPROPRIATIONS, SEPTEMBER 2013" because these support activities are felt directly by covered members of the Armed Forces. I want to make it clear that every DoD employee makes an essential contribution to the Department's ability to carry out its mission of defending the Nation. However, under this Act, we must determine who provides support to the members of the Armed Forces in active service, in a way that respects Congress's specific appropriation.

There are two distinct categories of civilian employees who fall within the scope of this statutory provision, in addition to those performing excepted activities. The first category includes those employees whose responsibilities provide support to service members performing active service and their families on an ongoing basis. The second category consists of those employees whose responsibilities contribute to sustaining capabilities and Force Readiness and which, if interrupted by the lapse in appropriations, will impact service members' ability to conduct assigned missions in the future. To fall within this second category, there must be a causal connection between the failure to perform the activity during the duration of an appropriations lapse and a negative impact on military members in the future. In other words, if the activity is not performed over the duration of an appropriations lapse, would it be possible to identify a negative impact that will be felt by military members at some time in the future? In undertaking this analysis, it should be assumed that regular appropriations will be restored within the near term.

Examples of activities that provide support to service members on an ongoing basis are:

i) *Health Care Activities and Providers;*
ii) *SAPRO, Behavioral Health, and Suicide Prevention Programs;*
iii) *Transition Assistance Programs for Military Members in active service;*
iv) *Family Support Programs and Activities;*
v) *Activities related to the repair and maintenance of weapons systems and platforms at the Operational and Intermediate level;*
vi) *Training Activities associated with military readiness;*
vii) *Supply Chain Management activities in support of near term Force Readiness;*
viii) *Human Resource Activities associated with organizing, equipping, manning and training functions;*
ix) *Installation Support and Facilities maintenance;*
x) *Commissary operations;*
xi) *Payroll activities;*
xii) *The provision of guidance or advice to military members when such guidance or advice is necessary for the military members to execute their functions (e.g., legal advice); and*
xiii) *Necessary support for all activities listed above, including legal, human resources, engineering, and administrative support.*

Examples of activities that contribute to capabilities and sustaining force readiness and that, if interrupted, would affect service members' ability to conduct assigned missions in the future include:

i) *Acquisition Program oversight and management (including inspections and acceptance), financial management, contract, logistics, and engineering activities, which support long term readiness;*
ii) *Activities related to the repair and maintenance of weapons systems and platforms at the Depot level;*
iii) *Supply chain management activities in support of long-term force readiness;*
iv) *Intelligence functions;*
v) *Information Technology functions; and*

vi) *Necessary support for all activities listed above determined to be within the scope of the Act, including legal, human resources, engineering, and administrative support.*

Employees performing these activities are within the scope of the Act only if a delay in the performance of these activities over the duration of a lapse in appropriations would have a negative impact on members of the Armed Forces in the future. Delays in the availability of new or repaired equipment would be one such impact.

Those employees of the Department who do not fall within the scope of the Act (unless they have been determined to be "excepted" and unless engaged in activities that support service members) include:

i) *CIO functions;*
ii) *DCMO functions, at the OSD and Component level;*
iii) *Legislative Affairs and Public Affairs functions not previously excepted or required in support of internal communications to members of the Armed Forces in active service;*
iv) *Auditor and related functions, not previously excepted, and DFAS functions that otherwise would not be determined to be "excepted" upon exhaustion of its working capital fund budgetary resources, and not required to process payrolls;*
v) *Work done in support of non-DoD activities and Agencies (except the U.S. Coast Guard); and Civil works functions of the Department of Army.*

As I stated above, all DoD employees perform work that is critical to the long-term strength of our Armed Forces, and our Nation. I fervently hope that the time will be short until I can recall all employees of the Department of Defense back to the vital work that they do helping to defend this Nation and secure our future. I will continue to explore all possibilities to this end. Those falling outside the scope of the Act include men and women who have devoted their lives to service of this country, and whose work on our behalf and on behalf of the Nation is enormously valuable and critical to the maintenance of our military superiority over the long term.

The Act provides appropriations for personnel; it does not provide appropriations for equipment, supplies, materiel, and all the other things that the Department needs to keep operating efficiently. While the Act permits the Department to bring many of its civilian employees back to work, and to pay them, if the lapse of appropriations continues, many of these workers will cease to be able to do their jobs. Critical parts, or supplies, will run out, and there will be limited authority for the Department to purchase more. If there comes a time that workers are unable to do their work, I will be forced once again to send them home.

Within the Office of the Secretary of Defense, the Under Secretary of Defense (Comptroller) will take the lead in overseeing the implementation of this guidance, assisted by other offices as necessary. Thank you all for your strong leadership at a very difficult time. The President, the country and I are all grateful for and depend on your leadership, courage, and commitment to our troops, their families and our country.

End Notes

[1] Military operations of the Department of Defense (DOD) are normally funded through annual appropriations provided in the DOD appropriations act and in the military construction, veterans' affairs, and related agencies appropriations act. DOD also administers a number of civil affairs activities that are funded in other appropriations bills, including civil construction projects managed by the Army Corps of Engineers. The non-military functions of the Department of Defense are not addressed in this report.

[2] The exception for national security was cited in OMB memos in 1980 and 1981 that are discussed below. Those memos, in turn, have been referenced by OMB guidance to agencies in years since then. OMB Circular A-11, which is periodically updated, also requires agencies to maintain plans for the orderly termination of operations in the event of a lapse in appropriations, with exceptions for personnel engaged in military, law enforcement, or direct provision of health care activities.

[3] For a general discussion of government shutdowns because of funding lapses, see CRS Report RL34680, Shutdown of the Federal Government: Causes, Processes, and Effects, coordinated by Clinton T. Brass.

[4] DOD, "Contingency plan memo," September 25, 2013.

[5] Statement of Secretary of the Treasury, Jacob J. Lew before the Senate Committee on Finance, "The Debt Limit," October 10, 2013; http://www.finance.senate.gov/imo/media/doc/10-10-013%20Final%20Written%20Testimony%20- %20Lew1.pdf.

[6] Deferrals under the Budget Control Act must be reported to Congress. This section is drawn largely from CRS Report CRS Report R41633, Reaching the Debt Limit: Background and Potential Effects on Government Operations, coordinated by Mindy R. Levit, pp. 9ff.

[7] Department of the Treasury, Financial Stability Oversight Council Chair, Eric M. Thorson, "Response to questions form Senator Hatch," OIF-CA-12-006, August 24, 2012; http://www.treasury.gov/about/organizational-structure/ig/Audit%20Reports%20and%20Testimonies/Debt%20Limit%20Response%20(Final%20with%20Signature).pdf.

[8] CRS Report RL34680, Shutdown of the Federal Government: Causes, Processes, and Effects, coordinated by Clinton T. Brass.

[9] H.R. 3210 was passed by 423 to 0 in the House on September 29, and by Unanimous Consent in the Senate on September 30, 2013.

[10] Active service is defined at 10 USC 101(d)(3). Active duty is defined at 10 USC 101(d)(1) to mean "full-time duty in the active military service of the United States. Such term includes full-time training duty, annual training duty, and attendance, while in the active military service, at a school designated as a service school by law or by the Secretary of the military department concerned. Such term does not include full-time National Guard duty." Full-time National Guard duty is defined at 10 USC 101(d)(5) to mean "training or other duty, other than inactive duty, performed by a member of the Army National Guard of the United States or the Air National Guard of the United States in the member's status as a member of the National Guard of a State or territory, the Commonwealth of Puerto Rico, or the District of Columbia under section 316, 502, 503, 504, or 505 of title 32 for which the member is entitled to pay from the United States or for which the member has waived pay from the United States."

[11] There is some ambiguity about how long this funding and authority would be available under H.R. 3210. Sec. 2 (a) refers to appropriations for FY2014 being available for "any period [italics added] during which interim or full-year appropriations for fiscal year 2014 are not in effect." At the same time, Sec. 3 provides that the appropriations and authority would be available "until whichever of the following first occurs": when appropriations are enacted, including a CR, or January 1, 2015, the end of the first quarter of FY2015; this language suggests that the authority could only be used once. See CRS Report R41948, *Automatic Continuing Resolutions: Background and Overview of Recent Proposals*, by Jessica Tollestrup.

[12] Memo available from author, Edward Liu.

[13] House Armed Services Committee, Subcommittee on Readiness, "Hearing on Implementation of the Pay Our Military Act," October 10, 2013.

[14] CBO, Cost Estimate of H.J.Res. 91, Department of Defense Survivor Benefits Continuing Appropriations Resolution, 2013, 10-1-013; http://www.cbo.gov/sites/default/files/cbofiles/attachments/hjres91.pdf.

[15] DOD, Deputy Secretary of Defense Ashton, B. Carter, " Guidance for Continuation of Operations in the Absence of Available Appropriations," September 25, 3013, http://www.defense.gov/home/features/2013/0913_govtshutdown/ Guidance-for-Continuation-of-Operations-in-the-Absence-of-Available-App.pdf; also Attachment, DOD," Contingency Plan Guidance for Continuation of Essential Operations in the Absence of Available Appropriations," September 2013, http://www.defense.gov/home/features/2013/0913_govtshutdown/Contingency-Plan-GuidanceAttachment.pdf; hereinafter, DOD, "Contingency plan memo," September 25, 2013.

[16] DOD, Secretary of Defense, Chuck Hagel, Memorandum for Subject: Components and Defense Agencies, "Guidance for Implementation of Pay Our Military Act," October 5, 2013; http://www.defense.gov/pubs/ Memorandum-Pay_Our_Military_Act_Guidance-FINAL.pdf.

[17] DOD, Transcript, Robert Hale, OSD/C, "Press Briefing on the Secretary of Defense's Interpretation of the Pay Our Military Act;" October 5, 2013; http://www.defense.gov/Transcripts/Transcript.aspx?TranscriptID=5320. According to testimony by Robert Hale, DOD Comptroller before the House Armed Services Committee on October 5, 2013, the 5% or about 40,000 defense civilians who would continue to be furloughed includes 35,000 DOD civilians working for the Corps of Engineers and the remainder working for the Department of Defense; see Department of Defense, Testimony of Robert F. Hale,

Undersecretary of Defense (Comptroller) before House Armed Services Committee, Subcommittee on Readiness, "Implementation of the Pay Our Military Act," October 10, 2013.

[18] DOD, Secretary of Defense, Chuck Hagel, Memorandum for Subject: Components and defense agencies,"Guidance for Implementation of Pay Our Military Act," October 5, 2013; http://www.defense.gov/pubs/MemorandumPay_Our_Military_Act_Guidance-FINAL.pdf.

[19] Ibid., p. 4

[20] H.R. 3210 provides that the act goes into effect after the Secretary makes a determination of which DOD civilians and contractor personnel would be covered; see Sec.2 (a)(2) and (3) in H.R. 3210.

[21] OMB, Office of Management and Budget, "Statement of Administration POLICY, "H.R. 3223—Federal Employee Retroactive Pay Fairness Act (House)," October 4, 2013; http://www.whitehouse.gov/sites/default/files/omb/legislative/sap/113/saphr3223h_20131004.pdf.

[22] See H.R. 3230 as passed by the House.

[23] CQ News, "Senate Democrats Rebuff 'Mini CR' Measures, by Sarah Chacko, CQ Roll Call, Oct. 3, 2013;http://www.cq.com/doc/news-4356141?from=bluebox&pos=bb10. OMB, "Statement of Administration Policy, H.J. Res. 70, 71, 72, 73 and H.R. 3230 – Limited Appropriations Resolutions, 2014 (Rep. Rogers, R-KY)," October 2, 2013; http://www.whitehouse.gov/sites/default/files/omb/legislative/sap/113/saphrj70-71-72-73_hr3230hr_20131002.pdf.

[24] Department of Defense, Under Secretary of Defense (Comptroller) Robert F. Hale, "News Briefing on the Department Of Defense's Plan for a Possible Government Shutdown," September 27, 2013; http://www.defense.gov/ Transcripts/Transcript.aspx?Transcript ID=5308.

[25] DOD, Memorandum for all Department of Defense Employees, "Guidance for Potential Government Shutdown," September 23, 2013.

[26] DOD, Memorandum for all Department of Defense Employees, "Potential Government Shutdown," September 26, 2013.

[27] OMB, Director Sylvia Burwell, M-13-22, Memorandum for the Heads of Executive Departments and Agencies, "Planning for Agency Operations during a Potential Lapse in Appropriations," September 17, 2013, http://www.whitehouse.gov/sites/ default/files/ omb/memoranda/2013/m-13-22.pdf.

[28] Department of Defense, News transcript, "Media Availability with Secretary Hagel on the Government Shutdown" October 1, 2013; http://www.defense.gov/Transcripts/ Transcript.aspx?TranscriptID=5314.

[29] Howard P. "Buck" McKeon, Chairman, House Armed Services Committee, "Letter to Chuck Hagel, Secretary of Defense, October 1, 2013, http://armedservices.house.gov/index.cfm/2013/10/mckeon-letter-to-hagel-on-pay-ourmilitary-act.

[30] H.R. 3210 was not considered in committee by either house so there are no reports indicating legislative intent.

[31] Congressman Mike Coffman, website,"House Passes Coffman Bill to Keep Military Paid," http://coffman.house.gov/ index.php?option=com_content&view=article&id=875:house-passes-coffman-bill-to-keep-military-paid&catid= 36:latest-news&Itemid=10.

[32] DOD, "Contingency plan memo," September 25, 2013.

[33] H.R. 3210; see also, Roll Call, "President Signs Military Pay Bill," by Connor O'Brien, September 30, 2013.

[34] DOD, "Contingency plan memo," September 25, 2013.

[35] DOD, "Contingency plan memo," September 25, 2013.

[36] Department of Defense, Under Secretary of Defense (Comptroller) Robert F. Hale, "News Briefing on the Department Of Defense's Plan for a Possible Government Shutdown," September 27, 2013DOD Contingency plan memo," September 25, 2013.

[37] Ibid.

[38] Ibid., p. 5 and p. 7.

[39] DOD, "Contingency plan memo," September 25, 2013. DFAS activities financed through reimbursements from other appropriations would also continue as long as those funds lasted.

[40] DOD, Transcript, Robert Hale, OSD/C, "Press Briefing on the Secretary of Defense's Interpretation of the Pay Our Military Act;" October 5, 2013; http://www.defense.gov/Transcripts/Transcript.aspx?TranscriptID=5320. In reviewing the applicable law in 1980 and 1981, the Attorney General concluded that agencies are "authorized by law" to incur obligations in advance of appropriations "for the administration of benefit payments under entitlement programs when the funds for the benefit payments themselves are not subject to a one-year appropriation." This reasoning is the basis on which Social Security Administration personnel are authorized to continue to process Social Security checks even when appropriated funds for the agency lapse. See Opinion by Attorney General Benjamin Civiletti, January 16, 1981.

[41] According to Army guidance cited later in this report, during a lapse in appropriations, "Funded and automatic reimbursable orders may be accepted consistent with receipt of current year funded reimbursable authority"—i.e., reimbursable activities may continue to the extent funds are available to provide the reimbursements.

[42] DOD, "Contingency plan memo," September 25, 2013, attachment, p. 8. DOD, Transcript, Robert Hale, OSD/C, "Press Briefing on the Secretary of Defense's Interpretation of the Pay Our Military Act;" October 5, 2013; http://www.defense.gov/Transcripts/ Transcript.aspx?TranscriptID=5320.

[43] The Feed and Forage Act does not itself permit pay of personnel, but a different statute provides one exception. Section 2201(c) of Title 10 U.S. Code allows funding for an increase in the number of active duty troops to be incorporated into the list of activities that may be funded under 41 U.S.C. 11—i.e., it indirectly expands the purposes for which funding under the Feed and Forage Act may be available. The provision applies only to funding for an increase in the number of active duty personnel, however, not to funding of current personnel levels.

[44] See U.S. Department of Defense, Office of the Under Secretary of Defense (Comptroller), "Budget Execution: Processes and Flexibility," March 2009, p. 17, http://comptroller.defense.gov/execution/ Budget_Execution_Tutorial.pdf, which says, with regard to the Feed and Forage Act: "These authorities require congressional notification and do not permit actual expenditures until Congress provides an appropriation of the requested funds." The tutorial also notes that the authority to fund an increase in personnel under 10 U.S.C. 2210 "is of limited value since it provides only for obligations and not for expenditures (payments to members)."

[45] The 2011 DOD guidance and 1998 Army shutdown guidance discussed in this mention the Feed and Forage Act as a potential source of authority, but neither discusses the circumstances under which it might be invoked.

[46] DOD, "Contingency plan memo," September 25, 2013.

[47] Office of Management, Director, "Memorandum for Heads of Executive Departments and Agencies," Agency Operations in the Absence of Appropriations," November 17, 1981, http://www.opm.gov/policy-data-oversight/payleave/furlough-guidance/attachment_a-4.pdf.

[48] The April 25, 1980 and January 16, 1981 Civiletti opinions and the September 30, 1980 OMB memorandum are available as appendices in U.S. General Accounting Office, Funding Gaps Jeopardize Federal Government Operations, GAO Report PAD-81-31, March 3, 1981, online at http://archive.gao.gov/f0102/114835.pdf. The other memoranda cited, except for the 2011 and 2013 OMB memos, are available online as appendices to Office of Personnel Management, "Guidance and Information on Furloughs," online at http://www.opm.gov/furlough/furlough.asp. The 2011 OMB memo is available at http://www.whitehouse.gov/sites/default/files/omb/memoranda/2011/m11-13.pdf., while the 2013 OMB memo is available at http://www.whitehouse.gov/sites/default/files/ omb/memoranda/2013/m-13- 22.pdf. Hereafter in this report, these opinions and memoranda are cited by author or agency and date. Other Department of Justice opinions related to operations in advance of appropriations have been issued as well.

[49] These provisions were formerly Sections 655(a) and 655(b) of Title 31, and were renumbered without substantive change in a recodification of Title 31 by P.L. 97-258, enacted on September 13, 1982. Attorney General opinions in 1980 and 1981 discussed in this memo refer to the earlier numbering. Section 1342 was also amended by P.L. 101-508, November 5, 1990. The current version of the Antideficiency Act reads, in part, as follows: § 1341. Limitations on expending and obligating amounts (a) (1) An officer or employee of the United States Government or of the District of Columbia government may not—make or authorize an expenditure or obligation exceeding an amount available in an appropriation or fund ...involve either government in a contract or obligation for the payment of money before an appropriation is made unless authorized by law; ....§ 1342. Limitation on voluntary services. An officer or employee of the United States Government or of the District of Columbia government may not accept voluntary services for either government or employ personal services exceeding that authorized by law except for emergencies involving the safety of human life or the protection of property.

[50] OMB, Director Sylvia Burwell, M-13-22, Memorandum for the Heads of Executive Departments and Agencies, "Planning for Agency Operations during a Potential Lapse in Appropriations," September 17, 2013, http://www.whitehouse.gov/sites/default/files/omb/memoranda/2013/m-13-22.pdf.

[51] There has been some discussion of the possibility that the military services could obligate funds for civilian pay for at least a month or so in advance, which would allow personnel to continue working and for pay checks to be issued for some time after a funding lapse. Such a prospect is at odds with longstanding procedures which require agencies to halt operations in the event of a funding lapse and for non-excepted personnel to be furloughed. Continuing resolution language stipulates that "only the most limited funding action of that permitted ... shall be taken in order to provide for continuation of projects and activities" (P.L. 111-242, Section 110), which would appear to limit such advance obligations.

[52] Office of Management, Director, Memorandum for Heads of Executive Departments and Agencies," Agency Operations in the Absence of Appropriations," November 17, 1981, http://www.opm.gov/policy-data-oversight/pay leave/furlough-guidance/attachment_a-4.pdf.

[53] This phrasing was initially used in a memorandum issued by OMB Director James McIntyre on September 30, 1980, and repeated in a November 17, 1981, memorandum by OMB Director David Stockman. Subsequent OMB memoranda in advance of anticipated

shutdowns refer to the 1980 and 1981 memoranda as guidance in preparing shutdown plans. See, for example, OMB Director Alice M. Rivlin, "Memorandum for Heads of Executive Departments and Agencies: Agency Plans for Operations during Funding Hiatus," OMB Memorandum M-95-18, August 22, 1995, available on line as Appendix A-1 at http://www.opm.gov/furlough/furlough.asp.

[54] DOD, Deputy Secretary of Defense Ashton, B. Carter, " Guidance for Continuation of Operations in the Absence of Available Appropriations," September 25, 3013, http://www.defense.gov/home/features/2013/0913_govtshutdown/ Guidance-for-Continuation-of-Operations-in-the-Absence-of-Available-App.pdf; also Attachment, DOD," Contingency Plan Guidance for Continuation of Essential Operations in the Absence of Available Appropriations," September 2013, http://www.defense.gov/home/features/2013/0913_govtshutdown/Contingency-Plan-GuidanceAttachment.pdf; hereinafter, DOD, "Contingency plan memo," September 25, 2013. For general background, see Shutdown of the Federal Government: Causes, Processes, and Effects, coordinated by Clinton T. Brass.

[55] Activities involving technical intelligence information collection, analysis and dissemination functions not in direct support of excepted activities (e.g., general political and economic intelligence unrelated to ongoing or contingency military operations, support of acquisition programs, support to operational test and evaluation, intelligence policy security promulgation and development, systems development and standards, policy and architecture) are not excepted activities.

[56] Activities in support of environmental requirements which are not necessary to prevent imminent threat to life or property are not excepted activities.

[57] Contingency planning in medical command headquarters not immediately necessary to support excepted activities is not an excepted activity.

[58] Elective surgery and other elective procedures in DOD medical and dental facilities are not excepted activities. Surgery to continue recovery of function/appearance of Wounded Warriors is an excepted activity.

[59] Installation education centers may continue to operate utilizing military personnel, so that private agencies such as colleges and universities may provide courses for which payment bas already been made. Civilian employees on TDY for training or education associated with non-excepted activities should be returned to their home stations as part of the orderly closedown of operations. Civilian personnel on PCS orders attending training or educational activities should remain in place.

[60] DODEA summer school activities are non-excepted activities.

[61] Activities funded entirely through NAF sources will not be affected. Military personnel may be assigned to carry out or support non-excepted MWR activities, where deemed necessary or appropriate, to replace furloughed employees.

[62] Preparation of financial reports, research and correction of problem disbursements, adjustments to prior-year funds (excepted as noted above) including those related to programs and contracts that do not support excepted activities, and approval of the use of currently available funds to pay obligations against closed accounts arc not excepted activities.

[63] DWCFs/RFs are not directly impacted by a lapse in annual appropriations. Management actions should be taken to sustain operations and minimize operational impact resulting from late approval of annual appropriations. Management actions which could be taken to conserve cash reserves include delay of training, minimal travel, reduction in supplies, and other actions consistent with management objectives. Inter-DWCF/RF billings will continue unless a suspension request is approved by the Office of the Under Secretary of Defense

(Comptroller), Approval may be requested for advance billing of funded customer orders. Plan guidance for excepted activities is applicable to DWCF/RF internal operations.

[64] DOD, Secretary of Defense, Chuck Hagel, Memorandum for Subject: Components and defense agencies," Guidance for Implementation of Pay Our Military Act," October 5, 2013; http://www.defense.gov/pubs/MemorandumPay_Our_Military_Act_Guidance-FINAL.pdf.

INDEX

A

access, 48, 50, 60, 61, 62, 67
accommodation, 2
accounting, 27
adjustment, 115
administrative support, 91, 118, 119
aerospace, 70
Afghanistan, 88, 92, 97, 100, 104, 109
agency actions, 7
agency decisions, 11
annual rate, 34, 38
Antideficiency Act, vii, viii, 1, 3, 4, 5, 6, 7, 10, 11, 15, 18, 20, 21, 23, 26, 28, 73, 75, 81, 87, 99, 101, 102, 103, 104, 105, 106, 107, 108, 124
appointees, 10
Appropriations Act, 9, 24, 82, 83, 116
armed forces, 90, 93, 94, 96
Asia, 66
assets, 21, 52, 62, 69
attachment, 21, 22, 23, 109, 123, 124
Attorney General, 4, 5, 20, 21, 74, 75, 96, 99, 103-108, 123, 124
audit, 98
authority(s), 4, 5, 6, 9, 10, 15, 19, 20, 21, 24, 25, 50, 61, 74, 76, 77, 78, 79, 80, 81, 83, 87, 88, 89, 93, 94, 96, 98, 99, 100, 101, 102, 104, 106, 107, 108, 109, 110, 111, 112, 113, 116, 117, 120, 121, 123

B

banking, 12, 108
bankruptcy, 11, 13
banks, 48
base, 97
basic research, 59, 61
beer, 48, 54
beneficiaries, 14, 15, 19, 68
benefits, 8, 15, 50, 51, 59, 60, 68, 69, 78, 87, 88, 89, 98, 106, 114
Big Bang, 62
blood, 63
breakdown, 58
budget cuts, 16
budget deficit, 78
budgetary resources, 119
Bureau of Labor Statistics, 34, 57
businesses, vii, 31, 49, 54, 56, 57, 64, 66

C

cash, 6, 38, 69, 88, 98, 115, 125
cash flow, 69
catastrophes, 64
CDC, 50, 51, 61
Census, 35, 39, 57
challenges, 70
chemical, 51, 63, 113
Chicago, 43

child labor, 65
childcare, 96
children, 50, 60, 64
citizens, 52, 69, 70, 109
civil service, 70
classes, 69, 80
cleanup, 68, 113
clinical trials, 50
closure, 13, 25, 67
clothing, 99, 114
clusters, 61
Coast Guard, 99, 119
coastal communities, 56
colleges, 125
commercial, 57, 61
commodity, 57
community(s), 13, 16, 29, 49, 56, 60, 68
compensation, 16, 19, 24, 25, 50, 57, 58, 70, 97
competitive advantage, 69
compliance, 26, 50, 63, 65
computer, 67, 97, 112
computing, 61
conference, 92, 93, 112
conflict, 2, 109
Congress, vii, ix, 1, 2, 3, 4, 5, 6, 7, 9, 10, 11, 15, 17, 18, 20, 21, 22, 23, 24, 25, 26, 27, 28, 29, 58, 73, 77, 78, 80, 82, 83, 85, 86, 88, 90, 92, 94, 95, 101, 107, 109, 111, 116, 117, 120, 123
congressional budget, 81
Congressional Budget Act of 1974, 81
congressional hearings, 13, 22, 26
consent, 55
Constitution, 3, 10, 26, 107
construction, 19, 38, 43, 45, 98, 120
consulting, 93
Consumer Price Index, 49, 57
consumption, 43
Continental, 113
contingency, 16, 22, 23, 26, 28, 83, 86, 88, 93, 94, 97, 103, 112, 125
continuous data, 62
contractor bills, ix, 85
cooling, 56

correlation, 39, 45
cosmetics, 63
cosmic rays, 62
cost, 14, 27, 41, 49, 50, 58, 67, 68, 72, 87, 90, 91
counsel, 16
counseling, 60, 113
covering, 43, 76
criminal investigations, 12
crises, 113
customers, 15

D

danger, 64, 111, 113
data structure, 41
deficit, 6
Department of Agriculture, 60, 70
Department of Commerce, 24, 54, 57, 70, 82, 83
Department of Defense, v, vii, ix, 16, 24, 29, 49, 52, 53, 58, 68, 70, 80, 82, 83, 85, 88, 89, 93, 94, 99, 102, 104, 116, 117, 119, 120, 121, 122, 123
Department of Education, 71
Department of Energy, 52, 68, 69, 71
Department of Health and Human Services, 70
Department of Homeland Security, 70, 80, 83
Department of Justice, 3, 20, 21, 71, 81, 87, 90, 93, 102, 103, 105, 117, 124
Department of Labor, 34, 35, 65, 71
Department of the Interior, 70
Department of the Treasury, 70, 120
Department of Transportation, 19, 24, 69, 71, 82, 83
deployments, 97
direct cost, 57
directives, 102
disability, 50, 51, 59, 67, 87
disaster, 12, 64, 108, 113
disaster assistance, 12, 108
disbursement, 7
discrimination, 65

diseases, 13
disposition, 65
distribution, 12, 45, 108, 113
District of Columbia, 24, 78, 79, 82, 83, 87, 92, 121, 124
DOJ, 3, 5, 7, 22, 25, 87
DOT, 69
downsizing, 23
drinking water, 63
drugs, 12, 49, 57

European Union, 66
evidence, 33
execution, 3, 17, 111, 123
executive branch, 6, 10, 11, 13, 16, 78, 80, 105
exercise, 10, 14, 111
expenditures, 101, 102, 103, 106, 123
explosives, 13
export promotion, 54
extracts, 63

E

economic activity, vii, 32, 33, 38, 43
economic development, 41
economic growth, 34, 38
economic growth rate, 34
economic indicator, 32, 38, 39
economic performance, 32, 33
education, 60, 125
EEOC, 65
emergency, vii, 1, 5, 12, 23, 25, 63, 98, 99, 100, 105, 108, 113, 114
emergency response, 99
employers, 67
employment, 4, 33, 34, 36, 39, 40, 41, 42, 45, 50, 60, 65, 97, 105, 108
employment growth, 34
enemies, 19
energy, 48, 54
enforcement, 12, 13, 51, 65, 67, 115
engineering, 70, 118, 119
enrollment, 61
environment, 26, 33, 43, 64, 70
environmental conditions, 62
environmental protection, 59
Environmental Protection Agency, 51, 71, 113
EPA, 51, 63, 70, 113
epidemiologic, 61
Equal Employment Opportunity Commission, 65, 71
equality, 41, 42
equipment, 12, 97, 99, 113, 119
equity, 55

F

FAA, 49, 56
families, 50, 52, 56, 60, 69, 88, 91, 101, 114, 117, 120
family support, 91, 98
FDA, 49, 50, 57, 63
FDA approval, 57
federal agency, 18, 103
Federal Communications Commission, 71
federal courts, 14, 15, 16
Federal Emergency Management Agency, 59
federal funding gaps, vii
federal funds, 75
federal government, v, vii, viii, 1, 2, 3, 5, 6, 8, 9, 10, 18, 19, 20, 21, 23, 24, 26, 28, 47, 68, 73, 75, 80, 81, 82, 83, 88, 120, 124, 125
Federal Judicial Center, 14
federal judiciary, 14, 15
federal law, 13
Federal Reserve, 21
FEMA, 59
financial, 19, 28, 55, 56, 62, 66, 67, 101, 102, 103, 104, 118, 125
Financial Crimes Enforcement Network, 66
financial institutions, 55
financial reports, 125
firearms, 13
fires, 60
fiscal year, viii, ix, 2, 3, 4, 21, 24, 59, 64, 73, 74, 75, 76, 78, 80, 81, 85, 88, 97, 101, 115, 116, 121

fish, 55
fisheries, 56
fishing, 48, 55
flammability, 64
flexibility, 96
flooding, 64
floods, 60, 64
food, 12, 49, 50, 59, 63, 92, 113, 114
Food and Drug Administration, 24, 49, 82
food products, 63
food safety, 50, 63
food services, 92, 113
foodborne illness, 50, 63
force, 91, 100, 118
forecasting, 45
formula, 15, 75
funds, viii, 3, 6, 10, 12, 14, 15, 19, 28, 52, 56, 60, 62, 69, 73, 87, 89, 96-111, 115, 116, 123, 124, 125
furloughs, vii, viii, 1, 8, 14, 15, 18, 22, 23, 25, 27, 47, 49, 50, 51, 52, 56, 58, 59, 61, 67, 69, 86, 88, 93, 94, 95, 96, 107

G

GAO, 4, 5, 20, 21, 23, 25, 26, 28, 81, 124
gas drilling, vii, 31
GDP, viii, 31, 32, 34, 38, 43, 47, 48, 53, 54
General Accounting Office, 19, 81, 124
General Services Administration, 71
Georgia, 60
global security, 18
goods and services, 66, 101, 102
government expenditure, 19
government procurement, 16
government shutdowns, vii, 1, 3, 14, 15, 81, 120
government spending, 48
governments, 21, 22, 66
graduate students, 63
grants, 21, 23, 61, 107
grass, 57
Gross Domestic Product, viii, 47
growth, viii, 31, 32, 33, 34, 35, 38, 39, 43, 47, 48, 53, 54, 58

growth rate, 31, 32, 33, 34, 43
guidance, 6, 8, 9, 11, 18, 22, 23, 25, 66, 81, 86, 87, 88, 91, 94, 95, 96, 97, 98, 99, 100, 101, 102, 103, 104, 105, 106, 107, 108, 109, 111, 116, 117, 118, 120, 123, 124, 125, 126
guidelines, 14, 16, 75, 100

H

hazardous materials, 12, 113
hazardous waste, 51, 63, 113
health, 13, 59, 61, 63, 64, 90, 91, 98, 114, 120
Health and Human Services, 24, 82, 83
health care, 91, 98, 114, 120
heating oil, 49, 57
heteroskedasticity, 40
hiring, viii, 13, 31, 70
history, 15, 28, 78, 89
homeland security, 29
homeowners, 48, 55
House, 10, 17, 20-27, 29, 75, 77, 78, 80, 82, 86, 87, 89, 90, 92, 94, 121, 122
House of Representatives, 10, 82
housing, vii, 31, 34, 38, 48, 55, 113
Housing and Urban Development, 24, 71, 82, 83
human, viii, 4, 5, 21, 62, 63, 73, 75, 81, 87, 88, 104, 105, 109, 111, 118, 119, 124
human resources, 118, 119
hypothesis, 41

I

ID, 122
identification, 110
idiosyncratic, 44, 45
immigration, 67
imported products, 63
income, 48, 52, 55, 60, 68, 69, 101
indirect effect, vii, 31
individuals, 18, 25, 29, 48, 50, 51, 55, 59, 66, 67, 80

industrial chemicals, 64
industry(s), vii, 13, 31, 49, 56, 62, 64
information technology, 23, 91
injury(s), 64, 65
inspections, 49, 50, 51, 59, 63, 64, 114, 118
inspectors, 64
institutions, 55
integrity, 51, 67
intelligence, 29, 91, 97, 99, 100, 112, 125
Internal Revenue Service, 48
international trade, 59
Intervals, 46
intervention, 113
investment, viii, 31, 49, 66
Iran, 66
issues, vii, 1, 2, 17, 18, 49, 59, 61, 92

J

job creation, 36, 43, 66
judicial branch, 10, 83
judicial power, 10, 14
judiciary, 10, 11, 14, 15, 16, 28

L

labor market, 34, 36
law enforcement, 29, 108, 112, 120
laws, 3, 14, 19, 65, 79, 94, 100
laws and regulations, 100
lawyers, 14, 93, 116
layoffs, 68
lead, 23, 32, 43, 64, 78, 106, 120
leadership, 25, 87, 92, 120
legislation, 2, 9, 19, 21, 24, 86, 88, 92, 94
lending, 48, 55
light, 5, 21
liquidate, 5, 6
liquidity, 89
loan guarantees, viii, 31
loans, 21, 48, 55, 60
local government, 113
logistics, 100, 114, 118
love, 70

M

magnitude, 58
majority, 15, 28, 58, 63, 64, 66
management, 91, 103, 113, 118, 125
manufacturing, 39
material handling, 113
materials, 25, 114
mathematics, 38
matrix, 44
matter, 74, 77
measurement, 41, 44
media, 13, 26, 83, 120
medical, 49, 51, 55, 57, 61, 63, 67, 87, 97, 99, 106, 108, 112, 113, 114, 125
medical care, 108
Medicare, 78, 88
medicine, 61
Mediterranean, 92
membership, 97
merchandise, 64
Mexico, 62
military, ix, 50, 52, 60, 68, 85-90, 92, 93, 94, 95, 96, 97, 98, 99, 100, 101, 102, 104, 106, 109, 110, 112, 113, 115, 116, 117, 118, 119, 120, 121, 122, 124, 125
minimum wage, 65
mission(s), 25, 52, 62, 65, 68, 69, 70, 91, 100, 117, 118
models, 32, 43, 45
morale, 86, 89, 91, 117
museums, 13, 87, 92

N

narcotics, 66
National Aeronautics and Space Administration, 51, 71
National Institutes of Health, 13, 50, 92
National Park Service, 13, 49, 51, 67
national parks, vii, 31, 49, 56, 57
National Response Team, 113

national security, ix, 12, 18, 29, 85, 86, 87, 88, 94, 97, 98, 99, 100, 102, 107, 110, 111, 112, 115, 120
natural disaster(s), 25, 29, 64, 111
natural gas, 49, 57
negative effects, 18
negotiating, 66
NOAA, 48, 55
Nobel Prize, 51, 61
NPS, 49, 56
Nuclear Regulatory Commission, 71
nuclear weapons, 52, 113

O

occupational health, 113
Office of Management and Budget, v, viii, ix, 5, 20, 21, 22, 47, 74, 75, 81, 85, 87, 88, 102, 122
officials, 3, 10, 13, 25, 66, 81
oil, vii, 31
OMB, ix, 5, 6, 7, 8, 9, 11, 14-18, 20-23, 26-29, 72, 85, 87, 88, 93, 96, 99, 102, 103, 105, 106, 107, 108, 120, 122, 124
OSHA, 64
outpatient, 12, 108, 114
outreach, 60
oversight, 17, 22, 23, 25, 63, 98, 118, 124
overtime, 65, 69

P

Pacific, 66
payroll, 9, 39, 40, 41, 49, 58, 72, 91
penalties, 89
Pentagon, 83
permission, 7, 55
permit, 4, 90, 105, 117, 123
personnel costs, 9
petroleum, 49, 57
physics, 61
plants, 68
platform, 62
police, 113

policy, 3, 16, 18, 22, 23, 25, 89, 107, 124, 125
pollution, 64
precedents, 16, 95, 102
preparation, 67, 108, 109
preservation, 12, 108
president, v, vii, 1, 2, 3, 6, 7, 8, 9, 10, 18, 20, 22, 24, 25, 27, 47, 58, 66, 70, 71, 77, 78, 81, 86, 87, 89, 90, 92, 93, 96, 107, 116, 120, 122
President Clinton, 9, 27, 78
President Obama, 89, 96
principal component analysis, 38
principles, 109, 117
prisoners, 12, 108
private sector, vii, 31, 54, 62, 70
procurement, 98, 101, 106
Producer Price Index, 57
professionals, 64
programming, 67
project, viii, 68, 73, 75
propane, 57
protection, viii, 4, 5, 12, 21, 58, 62, 73, 75, 81, 87, 88, 99, 104, 105, 107, 108, 109, 112, 113, 114, 115, 124
public health, 12, 49, 50, 59, 61, 108
public safety, 18
public service, 70
Puerto Rico, 121

R

radio, 27, 62
reactions, 87
reading, 117
real property, 113
reasoning, 106, 123
recall, 17, 86, 90, 91, 94, 117, 119
recalling, 58
recession, 38
recovery, 19, 29, 38, 125
recruiting, 69, 70, 97, 112
Reform, 17, 22, 23, 24, 26, 27, 29, 82
Registry, 49, 56
regression, 39, 40, 41, 42, 45

Index

regulations, 8, 68
relief, 65
remediation, 113
remittances, 102
rent, 6, 28
repair, 91, 97, 99, 113, 118
requirements, 10, 21, 25, 58, 97, 110, 112, 125
research facilities, 69
researchers, 51, 61, 62
reserves, 97, 115, 125
resolution, viii, ix, 9, 10, 16, 73, 74, 75, 77, 80, 90, 92, 124
resources, 16, 52, 68
response, 5, 15, 25, 29, 54, 64, 65, 74, 76, 78, 90, 113
restrictions, 15, 18
retail, 34, 35
retirement, 87, 89, 98
revenue, 48, 51, 55, 67
risk(s), 19, 64, 69, 70, 111

S

safety, viii, 4, 5, 12, 16, 21, 49, 58, 59, 64, 65, 73, 75, 81, 86, 87, 88, 90, 99, 104, 105, 107, 108, 109, 113, 114, 124
sample variance, 44
sanctions, 4, 66
savings, 28, 101
school, 63, 69, 98, 100, 121, 125
school activities, 125
science, 61, 62
scope, 57, 104, 108, 116, 117, 119
Secretary of Defense, 58, 86, 88, 90, 91, 93, 94, 108, 110, 112, 114, 120, 121, 122, 123, 125, 126
Secretary of the Treasury, 88, 120
security, 12, 18, 29, 61, 88, 99, 100, 107, 109, 112, 125
sellers, 55
Senate, 10, 20, 21, 23, 25, 75, 77, 78, 80, 82, 86, 87, 88, 90, 92, 120, 121, 122
sensitivity, 40, 41, 45
September 11, 25

services, vii, 3, 4, 11, 13, 15, 16, 18, 31, 32, 48, 49, 50, 53, 59, 60, 66, 67, 76, 86, 87, 88, 91, 98, 100, 101, 102, 104, 105, 106, 108, 111, 113, 114, 124
shortage, 6
significance level, 40, 41, 42
small businesses, vii, 31, 48, 49, 51, 55, 56, 64
Social Security, 3, 15, 17, 48, 51, 55, 58, 67, 71, 88, 106, 123
Social Security Administration, 15, 51, 58, 71, 106, 123
solution, 44
species, 56
spending, viii, 3, 31, 49, 53, 54, 56
SSA, 15, 28, 51, 55, 67
SSI, 15, 51, 67
stability, 52, 69, 115
stakeholders, 18
standard error, 40, 42
state(s), 3, 40, 43, 44, 45, 48, 49, 50, 54, 56, 57, 60, 62, 63, 64, 69, 113
statistics, 42
statutes, 4, 12
statutory provisions, 3
steel, 38, 40
stock, 98
storage, 49, 57, 113, 114
structure, 120
subsistence, 99, 114
substance abuse, 113
supervisors, 93
suppliers, 89
support services, 12, 97, 113
support staff, 16
Supreme Court, 11, 26
surveillance, 12, 13, 50, 61, 97, 112
suspensions, 68
syndrome, 57
Syria, 66

T

talent, 70
TAP, 60

tax collection, 12, 108
taxpayers, 66, 67
technology, 28, 56
telecommunications, 112
telephone, 15, 36, 66
territory, 121
terrorism, 112
terrorist organization, 66
testing, 13, 56, 67
threats, 113
time series, 43
tobacco, 13
tornadoes, 60
total costs, 27
tourism, 13, 49, 56
tracks, 38, 39
trade, 39, 48, 54, 66
trade agreement, 66
training, 91, 92, 94, 96, 97, 100, 110, 112, 114, 115, 118, 121, 125
trajectory, 33
transactions, 67
transfusion, 63
transparency, 18
transport, 12, 69
transportation, 12, 19, 48, 54, 99, 113, 114
Treasury, ix, 3, 6, 12, 24, 48, 53, 54, 65, 82, 83, 85, 88, 89
treaties, 112
trust fund, 19, 89, 106, 111

U

U.S. Army Corps of Engineers, 113
U.S. Geological Survey (USGS), 56
unemployment insurance, 32, 34, 36
uniform, 45
United, v, 12, 14, 47, 52, 61, 62, 66, 68, 82, 99, 104, 113, 121, 124
United States, v, 12, 14, 47, 52, 61, 62, 66, 68, 82, 99, 104, 113, 121, 124
universities, 125
updating, 22

USGS, 64

V

variables, 36, 40, 42, 43
vector, 43, 44, 113
vehicles, 113
venue, 65
veto, 9, 92
Vietnam, 99
vocational rehabilitation, 60
volatility, 32

W

wage payments, 65
wages, 65
war, 87, 88, 92, 94, 97, 109
warning systems, 112
Washington, 13, 20, 21, 22, 23, 24, 25, 26, 27, 28, 29, 70, 72, 82, 83
water, 51, 56
waterways, 12
weapons, 118
websites, 16, 17
welfare, 13, 78
well-being, 86, 91, 117
White House, 24, 27, 92
windows, 7, 33
witnesses, 22
worker rights, 59
workers, ix, 39, 52, 58, 64, 65, 72, 78, 85, 120
workforce, viii, 47, 58, 63, 69, 93, 94, 117
working conditions, 65
working families, 60
workplace, 49, 59, 64, 65

Y

young people, 60